Instagram Marketing

Step by Step Guide on Instagram
Advertising. How to Promote and Sell
Anything Through Instagram

Author

Contents

Introduction

The internet and digital media have paved the way for a world of opportunities. It is a world where you can sell anything so long as you have the right idea and desire to make cash.

With the advent of Instagram and other channels of social media, anyone can create a brand and make themselves known. You can advertise your business, products, and services and become a leader in your field. However, the sad news is that you can't get the success you desire just by posting appealing images. No, it goes beyond that, and there are a lot of things you need to learn to ensure this. Nonetheless, this does not mean it is far from your reach.

In the chapters to follow, you will learn all there is to know about Instagram. You will learn what Instagram is, why it is vital for your brand, and how to create a good business account. This is not all; you will also learn the best software for scheduling posts and how to make money via Instagram among a range of others.

More importantly, you will learn to create Instagram ad campaigns for the best reach and use stories and contests to help you sell your products and services to your audience. This and many more are what we will break down in this book.

I do not promise you that it will be an easy task. Attaining success on Instagram is not without its problems. However, I am confident that when you are through with this book, you will have detailed knowledge of how to be successful on Instagram.

Researching this book has been fun to do. I hope you will find it entertaining and easy to understand while reading.

Now, let us begin this fantastic journey.

Chapter 1

Instagram Basics

At some point, you may have come across the name Instagram. This is most likely the case even if you have no active profile. That is just how recognized Instagram has become today. One of the major perks of Instagram are the various photo filters, which when used on a typical image, makes it seem like it was professionally edited. There are filters which can make your pictures black and white, while others can boost the colors in the photos.

Although Instagram filters transformed editing on mobile devices for many of us, that is not all it has to offer. This application has a user base of more than 50 million! Remarkable right? What's more, it was able to attain this feat while on Android and iOS devices. When Instagram kicked off, in just six days, there were more than 4 million downloads! (Taylor, 2012).

The success of the app drew the attention of one of the most recognized social platforms in the globe: Facebook. On the 9th of April, Instagram was acquired for $1 billion by Facebook. Instagram has covered a lot of ground in terms of business since its introduction in 2010(Price, 2012). However, the app remains one of the easiest to use to date.

If you are not yet on Instagram, it is not a problem. In this chapter, we will be learning all the essentials to ensure you can set yourself up and get things running. But first, let's look further into Instagram.

What Is Instagram?

Instagram is a platform for social networking, which was designed around the sharing of videos and photos. It was initially kicked-off on iOS in October 2010. In April 2012, it was released for Android devices.

Similar to a majority of social media applications, Instagram gives you the capacity to follow individuals you have an interest in. When you do this, it develops a feed on your homepage where you can see recent posts from those you follow. You will also have the capacity to comment on posts and like them. Instagram also offers support for Stories, which is similar to Snapchat. With Stories, you can post a picture or set of images and video clips. These will be visible to others for a 24hour period before it expires and vanishes.

Additionally, Instagram lets you send direct messages to others privately. You can also check out their profiles to view things that interest you. So how does Instagram work? We will be learning how below, but first, you need to learn to create an account.

Creating an Instagram Account

The first step to take when it comes to creating an Instagram account is to download the application. If you use an Android phone, head to the Google Play store. If you are an iOS user, check out the App store. In any of these stores, run a search and instantly download.

After you have downloaded the application, you can now begin. All you have to do is select the camera icon. For those who don't want to download the app, there is not a problem. You can open Instagram on your desktop. However, there is a limitation to the number of actions you can perform on your desktop as opposed to your mobile device.

Now that you have covered this, the next step is to sign up.

Sign Up

It is mandatory for you to provide some information before you sign up. However, you are privy to a few choices which we will cover below:

- **Offer Your Mobile Number**: Here, you need to input your number, and you will be on your way to creating your account. If this is your first time of using the platform, this may be the ideal method of signing up. This info will always be accessible to you, and it will be less challenging to log in.

- **Use an Email Address**: If you already have an account on Instagram, this might be a good option for you, since you will be able to utilize a different email address. Receiving notifications is also seamless if you have more than one account, and you want to keep them separate.

- **Sign-up using Facebook**: For those who already have an account on Facebook, this is a fast and straightforward method of signing up and finding those you know who are already on Instagram. You will get immediate access to your list of friends, and you will be able to see those who are on Instagram. This makes it less difficult to follow those you know.

All of these methods can help you sign up with ease, so all you need is to choose the one that suits you best. After signing up, you can then move to the next step of picking a username.

Choose a Username

The username you choose is a very vital aspect of creating a new account on Instagram. Picking an account name can be very unnerving for many, but don't forget that it is something you can change any moment you want.

Knowing this, usernames are a very vital aspect of Instagram. A good name can help make your account unique and even help increase your follower count. The name you choose is dependent on what the account is for. As a rule of thumb, select a username that people can search for with ease. We will be taking a more in-depth look into usernames further in this book.

Select a Profile Picture

After you have carefully picked a username, now you need a picture on your profile. If it is an account for personal use, pick a great selfie. If your account is for business, choose one that explains what you do. If you like, you can also go with graphics. The idea is to use something you are comfortable with.

Any picture you decide to go with will be what users see first. Anytime you make an upload on Instagram, your profile picture will be right beside it. For this reason, you need to be careful when choosing a profile picture. Having selected your ideal profile picture, you can now follow those you know.

Start Following Those You Know

After putting your new account in place, it's time to start using Instagram. Look for the accounts of your friends and other accounts that you may have an interest in and begin to hit the follow button.

Ensure those you share a relationship with know that you now have an Instagram profile. The instant you begin to follow people; you will certainly get a follow back. In no time, you will have a successful Instagram account. Now that you have created your account, we will be looking into how it works, to ensure you can easily find your way around the platform.

Instagram- How Does It Work

After you have signed up and followed individuals, as we explained above, your Home tab will become quite active. Here, you will view posts from individuals and friends you have followed. Above, you will be able to see new stories uploaded by your friends. With a single tap, you can begin viewing the stories.

To send a direct message to other users, you can select the **Messages** icon. Tap it to begin a new message or check out the messages you presently have.

Making Posts on Instagram

To add a new post, all you need to do is to hit the **Plus** icon which you can find at the center of the toolbar beneath. Here, you can decide to take a new video or picture. You can also pick one image from your gallery or include many photos in a single post.

Once you have taken your picture, you can use one of the various filters offered by Instagram to edit your photographs. Lastly, you can include a comment to your uploads, tag those you know, include the locations if you desire, and decide if you want to send your uploads to other social platforms. The instant you hit the **Share** button, your picture will show up on your profile and the feeds of your followers. However, if you understand how to make posts on Instagram, and don't know the features at your disposal, you may not be able to take advantage of all the platform has to offer.

Features of Instagram

Instagram has included tons of features since its inception, which can be of benefit to marketers. Below are a few of the important ones that you have at your disposal.

Video Features

Similar to the typical photos posts, Instagram offers a video post feature. These video uploads are 60 seconds long. You can include a caption and filter. You can also tag your location before you upload the post.

In contrast to photos, video posts draw in more engagement from users. For brands or individuals who want to get ahead of the new Instagram algorithm which leverages the user engagement of your posts to decide if to show your content of the feed of users or not, this can offer huge potential.

Live Video

Live video has a concept which is different from the video posts. However, it is a fantastic feature to take advantage of. Here, followers are sent a push notification which informs them that you are about to go live. If followers click on the notification, they are redirected to your live video stream where they can like or leave comments in real time.

However, the instant you end the live stream, the video vanishes. For marketers looking to develop brand uniqueness and transparency, which are both vital on Instagram now, this is another effective method.

Mute Accounts

This feature allows you to mute post notifications from accounts of your choice. It is convenient in situations where you don't want to unfollow the said account. Also, this feature can help you keep up with your top accounts without any disruptions from accounts you don't want to view. It offers you control over the posts that show up on your feed.

IGTV

Instagram TV is an application you can find on Instagram. It offers users the capacity to share videos that are up to 60 minutes in length – similar to a TV episode. This can be very useful for individuals involved in video content creation which is one of the fastest rising innovations in content marketing, as more than 80 percent of businesses have begun tapping into the viability of video marketing.

Emoji Slider Polls

Now, you can use emojis to run polls. This new feature allows you to use emojis to let users take a poll on something they like or dislike.

If you are a marketer, there are a host of possibilities to this. You can upload an upcoming product in various colors and ask users to give it a rating. That way, you will know what the users want even before you decide to release. Doing this can save businesses a considerable amount of costs.

Stories

Like we covered above, the stories feature shares many similarities to Snapchat. Lots of users enjoy using stories which have led to a lot of updates. Below are some of the various ways you can use stories.

- **Mention Other Users**: Now, you can mention or tag other users in your stories. Just use the @ to find whomever you want to tag. You can integrate the mentions to stories or include them on the images. It can be used in tagging locations or those you know. When you are tagged by another user in their stories, you will get notified via your DM, and you will then have the capacity to upload the user's story as well.

- **Add Shoppable Tags to Stories**: Do you sell products or services? With this feature, you can tag your products in your stories. For instance, say you sell basketball shorts –you will tag the shorts in your stories so users can click and make direct purchases. This can help advertise your products in a user-generated or live action content.

- **Upload More Than One Story**: Now, you can upload videos and photos in bulk to your stories. If you are a marketer or social media marketer, this can save you tons of time as you will be able to upload ten images or videos simultaneously.

The features above are only a few of what Instagram offers. Take advantage of them today and make your marketing efforts more effective. Knowing these, let's delve into some of the other benefits you stand to gain from using Instagram for marketing.

Benefits of Instagram for Marketing

Instagram offers tons of perks to marketers, businesses, and individuals alike. Below are some of these fantastic benefits:

Lots of Individuals Are Utilizing Instagram

Instagram presently has more than 800 million active users, which is a massive amount if you look at it from a business perspective. From these millions of individuals, more than 50 million use the platform each day, with over 70 percent of them in other locations besides the United States (Balakrishnan & Boorstin, 2017). What's more, millennials make 34 percent of this number, and 38 percent of these visitors visit the site more than once every day (Clarke, 2019). With the vast amount of users, a business with the right Instagram strategy can attain colossal success.

Various Businesses Can Flourish

With access to this vast number of users, businesses are provided with infinite possibilities. This applies to established organizations as well as one-man companies. However, even for companies that are highly recognized, success is not an overnight task. Nonetheless, if a marketing team has the right strategy and is serious about getting visibility for their business, it is not impossible. They can make this happen by retaining an active presence on Instagram and posting at least once each day. This is the same way recognized brands like Adidas and Coca-Cola have attained vast levels of success using Instagram ("Social Media Case Studies & Client Stories | Sprout Social", 2019).

You Can Make Money On Instagram

Instagram has undergone many changes over the years. Now, more emphasis is placed on earning cash using product placement. With the shoppable posts, you can include tags to your products in uploads with links consisting of the price, product description and the capacity to make a purchase using the 'shop now' button, which directs users to your eCommerce store.

Using this easy feature, you can use the Instagram platform to get real sales. More than 70 percent of the users on Instagram stated that they purchased products via the platform, which makes it something worth taking advantage of (Smith, 2019).

It offers Stories

Instagram offers you the opportunity to let prospective clients know that there is a face behind your brand. You can do this using one of the numerous features you can access on the application; however, to make a lasting impression, stories, and live posts can do the trick. By using stories to take users on a walk behind-the-scenes of your organization and the individuals you work with, you can make your brand more relatable. A way of doing this is to post videos that show the way products are created, live Q&A sessions between your audience and yourself, among others.

The live post feature offered by Instagram is also an excellent way for you to build trust, credibility, and trust with the individuals who follow you. It could also help your brand feel less robotic and show that your business has a more human side. If your clients can see that you are more than just a corporation in search of ways to get their money, then it can help build your trust with them.

Collaborate with Influencers

If you have not heard the term before, Influencers are individuals with huge reach and credibility online, that can raise your brand's awareness with ease.

A skilled influencer can help increase your organization's returns because they have access to a target market in your niche that you won't usually have. If you can collaborate with an established influencer, they can aid in spreading the word of your product, services, or organizations to millions of individuals with only a few posts.

You can Enhance your visibility with Hashtags

As a newcomer in a particular sector, your competition may rattle you. However, if you properly implement hashtags, you can make your business stand out from the others.

Hashtags are similar to keywords. They help explain the message your post is trying to pass across. Well-known hashtags like #ShareaCoke by Coca-Cola have made waves in the industry and have made it even easier to love and recognize these brands.

You don't have to be a massive brand like Coca-Cola, but if you can efficiently implement hashtags, it can make a massive difference in helping your business stand out.

Engaging with Customers is Easy

What better way can you ingrain your business in the mind of clients? How about the chance to interact with them daily? Individuals love to air their opinions; it is a known fact, particularly if they like something. Instagram is a channel for users to comment on, like, and share their top posts.

The higher the number of comments and likes you get; the more visibility your organization gets. Increasing your number of likes is straightforward too. You can do this by taking pictures of high-quality, collaborating with other similar brands and using hashtags.

It is Mobile

In contrast to other platforms like Twitter and Facebook, which launched as sites based on browsers, Instagram began as an application from the beginning. Since over 80 percent of the time individuals spend on mobile is used on apps, your organization can exploit this and ensure your viewers can access your posts with ease on the move anywhere they are through Instagram.

People who use smartphones prefer Instagram because it does not have the disorderly view Facebook tends to have. Also, you will want to exploit this because it has been reported that Instagram engagement is more than ten times that of Facebook. This is undoubtedly a wide margin that can make a lot of difference to your marketing efforts.

Monitor the Competition

Your organization can watch its competition with the help of Instagram and observe the way they relate with the individuals who follow them. Observe carefully to learn the frequency at which they post, the content they post and how they relate with their followers. You can use what you learn to better define your strategy, and stay ahead of the competition.

It Provides You with Numerous Ways to Be Creative

Instagram offers you the opportunity to get creative. On Instagram, you can try out various strategies to come up with new ways to attract attention and add new customers and followers. You can prove to your followers that there is a personality behind your brand, and shopping with you can be a great experience. You can do this by combining shoutouts, contests, interactive videos, and vivid images, among others.

Link with Facebook

As we covered earlier, Instagram was purchased by Facebook for a whopping sum of $1 billion. For businesses who want to combine their marketing efforts on both platforms, this purchase came with a lot of opportunities.

Facebook and Instagram ads share a lot of similarities, and now that they are typically the same company, you can now run the same ad on Instagram and Facebook simultaneously. What this implies is that the instant you run an ad on any of these platforms, you can instantly double your reach.

Instagram Offers Great Analytics

With Instagram, measuring your success is very easy. Similar to other platforms, it allows you to keep track of your follower counts, levels of engagements, among others. However, Instagram takes it a little further by providing you with comprehensive analytic reports. These can aid you in interpreting the outcome of your ad campaigns with ease. With these analytics, you will be able to quickly pinpoint the kinds of posts on Instagram that offer the best results, so you can keep using them for continuous success.

It is a known fact that creating a new account on Instagram can be a scary process for many people. However, it can also be an enjoyable process, as well. Also, with the number of individuals taking advantage of this platform continually on the rise, you will be ignoring a massive amount of prospective clients if you are not on this platform. Start building your brand today, and you will have no regrets you did. What if you have no brand yet and want to begin? We will be exploring how you can do this in the next chapter.

Chapter 2

Creating Your Instagram Brand

Almost anyone can develop a brand on Instagram nowadays. However, developing a memorable brand that users would want to follow is something much more complex. This, on its own, is a technique that needs to be learned.

In this chapter, we will cover how to create a memorable brand for yourself on Instagram. Below are the steps that can help:

Define Your Objectives

The first thing you need to do even before making any post is to determine the reason you want to build your brand on the platform.

What are your objectives? What do you plan to achieve using Instagram?

Do you want to:

- Spread brand awareness?

- Find new clients?

- Try to build a community?

- Connect with existing customers?

- Enhance traffic to your blog?

- Enhance your impression on social media?

Depending on the type of brand you wish to build, your goals and objectives can differ. However, you can alter your goals as you grow.

Determine your Focus

After establishing your objectives, the next step is to determine your theme or focus on Instagram. Many brands make the error of having no focus and make random posts on Instagram. This will fail because you won't be able to make yourself unique from the others.

Locate a focus that aligns with your personality and stick to it. Your focus should also align with your brand. Try to have a direction from the start; your goal should be to let your followers know you and the services you offer. If you are at a loss as to what theme to be, all you need to do is get inspiration from Instagram by running a search. There are a lot of amazing accounts which will inspire you.

Define Your Theme

Your theme is your style on Instagram. It is one you stick with all through the time you use Instagram. Some users stick with a neutral only style, while some would prefer a darker style. For others, they choose to include funny posts after every three posts. If you want to be unique, its best to combine things a bit.

Consistently Release High-Quality Content

Posting frequently on social media platforms is essential, and the same applies to Instagram. If you desire to be unique, you need to publish content often.

To make things easier, you can use a tool to schedule posting as we covered in the previous chapter. As a rule of thumb, it is best to have content that would last you for no less than two weeks in place, before you begin. If you have new content you want to post, you can push it ahead in your scheduling tool.

Stay Active

To have a great brand on Instagram, you have to build a community. You can only do this if you are active.

Easy ways of doing this include:

- Commenting on the profile of others

- Following other people

- Liking the pictures of other users

These may seem basic, but it is a strategy that is certain to provide results.

Leverage Hashtags

To have the most impact, you have to take advantage of hashtags. If you can, take advantage of all 30 hashtags. If you are unaware of the hashtags to utilize, you can check out what your competitors or established influencers in your field are using.

It is vital to use hashtags because it offers exposure when individuals are going through hashtags to view pictures.

Develop a Branded Hashtag

A branded hashtag is one that you create for yourself. Putting one in place is a fantastic way to develop engagement instantly. A branded hashtag is when users utilize your hashtag to get an opportunity to feature on your Instagram account.

Many users enjoy tagging pages and utilizing hashtags on Instagram to be featured on a specific page. It is an excellent means of getting more followers and exposure.

The first step is to state it on your profile that anyone who uses your hashtag will get featured on your page. Then, look for a hashtag which is a bit popular with lower than 50k posts, head to those pictures and begin to like them. It is an excellent way of ensuring people notice your page. This will urge your followers and the individuals whose pictures you liked, to post images using your hashtags in a bid to feature on your page.

Reuse Content Published by Other Accounts

This is another excellent option if you don't want to utilize branded hashtags. Look for posts that are similar to your style and repost them on your page. In doing this, you can increase engagement and create connections with other users simultaneously.

To make sure the image quality is terrific, contact these individuals to get the authority to post their content on your account. Let them send you a picture of high-quality. This way, you get a good picture while creating connections too.

Search for Branded Accounts and Hashtags

If you want exposure, an effortless way is to locate accounts or branded hashtags in the same industry as you to get featured on.

An easy way of doing this is to run a search for a popular hashtag your demographic uses, and find out if they have used or tagged any hashtags to get a feature.

If you share how-to's on your account, you are not alone. Numerous accounts share how-to's from others. Keep an eye out for them. To go further, you can contact them via their Instagram DM to get them to notice you.

Collaborate with Other Accounts

A great way of branding your account and growing it at the same time is to collaborate with accounts that have similar engagement and following as yours. It is also recognized as a shoutout for shoutout.

This typically works this way; When you make a post, on the caption you put something in the lines of "If you want more amazing pictures like this, follow this account @user."

The account you are collaborating with also does the same thing, and you both get followers who are interested in what you do.

How to Choose a Great Instagram Name?

Determining the best Instagram username can be very complex; however, it is quite significant. It portrays the identity you are trying to pass along and also presents your content

These steps below can aid you in selecting an Instagram name that is simple, unique, appealing, and available.

Determine Your Context

When it comes to picking an Instagram username, a very vital step is to determine what you plan on doing with your Instagram account. Are you developing a personal Instagram page to post images of exotic locations you visit? Or are you picking a username for your business or blog? You need to determine what your plan is before you can effectively choose an Instagram username.

Pick the Components

If your goal is to post personal pictures for your family and loved ones to see, you may want to include the following components: first name, middle, and last name. You also want to add any nickname you might have alongside your date of birth.

If your goal is to create an account for your business, you may want to integrate your business name, the kind of business, the business location, and the keywords common in its field. Using the same username on all your business social media pages is a great idea. The instant you choose a username, ensure that is the same one you use for Twitter, Facebook, and if possible, your email.

Mix Things Up

Having determined the components, you want to incorporate in your user name, try to shake things up to see which of the arrangement seems better. You want to go with a username that is not difficult to remember, sounds great when read aloud and looks great when typed out. For a business Instagram username, it is especially critical to pick one that is easy to remember. Don't pick one with many numbers because users would likely not recognize. Also, make sure you don't use any information that can be used to identify you, like your address or phone number. You don't want random users on Instagram to begin ringing up your line because you uploaded it on Instagram.

Other Things to Avoid

Avoid underscores. Finding this symbol on the keyboard can be so tedious. Also, when you use more than one underscore at the same time, it can be hard to point out the numbers.

Don't copy the Instagram username of another user with only one letter being different. Users would be unable to tell you apart, and that user may not find this appealing.

Ensure it is not too lengthy. It is difficult to type out or remember lengthy usernames. Use something memorable and brief.

Check If your Chosen Username Is Available

After you have selected a few usernames, you need to check if they are available. You can use a tool for this or run a search for the username to determine if there is a username similar to it. If it is not available, you can use punctuation. Instagram supports punctuation differences, and they can sometimes make your handle more legible.

You have the luxury to try as many usernames as possible. And the instant you have determined your component, there are a host of combinations you can use. The moment you have a few options that you have proven to be available, you can say them out loud and pick the best sounding one.

If it does not work out, and you go with a name you dislike, later on you can change it without any impact on your account. If you want to use another username, head to your profile, and hit "edit profile." When doing this, repeat the steps from the start and experiment with new usernames. Also, remember to find out if these names are in use. You don't want to pick a name and learn later that it is in use.

If you have a great brand, but your profile/bio is in a mess, you may never get the reach you desire. This makes it a vital reason to learn to create a good bio that attracts people. The next chapter will cover this in more detail.

Chapter 3

How to Create A Great Bio

Many individuals who use Instagram for marketing tend to make the mistake of ignoring their profile/bios. For the ones who do remember, their bio is something they fill in a rush when they create their accounts.

However, this should not be the case. Your bio is a significant aspect of your page, which is the first thing visitors see. It passes vital information regarding your business, establishes a great first impression for your business and transforms individuals who visit your profile into visitors and ultimately, customers.

For this reason, you need to understand how to make your profile catchy and appealing as this will help you get the best from your account on Instagram alongside your efforts in marketing. What else can you do? That is what we will be covering in this chapter. First, we will be looking at the basics.

Instagram Bio – What is it?

Your Instagram bio, like we covered earlier, aids in describing you and your business. It is the first thing visitors come across. Instagram offers you 150 characters to utilize in your bio. Also, you will be allowed to add one external link. There is also additional input for your username, which has an extra 30-character length. With this in mind, what does your bio have to achieve?

What Should Your Instagram Bio Achieve?

- There are a lot of things your profile/bio should accomplish. They may seem like a lot considering you are restricted to a specific number of characters. Nonetheless, a great Instagram bio has to cover the following:

- Show vital information about your business, like the name of your brand, industry, and so on. You can change this at any time via your profile settings.

- Offer users on Instagram with a means of reaching you.

- Display the personality of your brand, ensuring your style and voice aligns with your website and any other social platforms you may have.

- Determine your unique selling point, to aid your target audience, interpret why your brand is relevant to them

- Push relevant actions like viewing or sharing content, heading to the website to buy a product, leave a comment, or follow back.

The good news is that Instagram offers you a range of features that you can utilize along with your bio. With these features, you can easily cover the essential profile considerations, which will aid users in understanding your business and what you do, to enable you take additional steps.

Now, we will be taking a look at how to make an exceptional Instagram bio.

Take Advantage of Keywords

If you hit "Edit Profile", "Name" is the first area you will find. It is not the same as your Username, which is what creates the URL of your Instagram profile. It offers your page its name.

The initial 30 characters of your bio is made up of the name field, and it can go a long way in your Instagram SEO efforts. When individuals run a search for something on Instagram, it analyzes the words used in the Name field for a fit. So if your goal is to have a good ranking when it comes to Instagram SEO, you need to take advantage of keywords that are significant to your niche by including them in the Name field. If you can, try to include emojis in the Name field as people tend to run a lot of searches on them.

Writing Your Bio

Your Instagram bio hugely affects your audience. From a glance, people should be able to understand what your business is all about and why they are relevant to you. The bio should also have the capacity to lure people to follow you, and finish a specific action you desire like follow a website, or make a purchase.

You need to try to fit in as much data as you can, concerning your brand in the allocated 150 characters. This can be a tedious task considering the tight character limit. Due to this, we will be covering some of the vital information that should be included in your bio;

- Precise Service or Niche: If you belong to a particular industry niche or profession, or you are known to provide a specific service, then it is vital to make this evident in your Instagram bio so you can connect instantly with the appropriate crowd.

- Experience and Skills: By letting your audience know your level of expertise and what you can do, it will be easy to build trust with them, while providing them with a look into the services you render.

- Interests and Hobbies: If your brand is dependent on you as a person, then it is vital for you to develop a connection with your audience. Tell them a little about your interests, who you are, beliefs, and values so you can present yourself as engaging and captivating.

- Add a little humor to your brand's voice: It is vital to use the voice of your brand, as doing this will make sure you stay consistent on every social network and allow your audience to recognize you instantly. However, including a bit of humor will make it easier to relate to your brand.

You need to consider a host of things when you are putting together your Instagram bio. However, there are a lot of things you need to incorporate. Below are a few other components you need to add to develop a great bio

Take Advantage of Hashtags

Including a branded hashtag in your bio is another essential Instagram technique. In addition to creating a community for your brand, it will also aid you in driving post engagement. For instance, Airbnb efficiently utilizes its branded hashtag in its bio and even uses it to urge user-generated content.

When you offer your followers the means to distribute their content with your community using your branded hashtag, it will be less challenging to develop an engaging Instagram page. This can aid you in promoting your company and ensuring your brand gets to a broader audience.

Include Emojis

A great way to give your profile an exciting and authentic look, while ensuring your brand is unique, is to include emojis.

What's more, emojis don't require the same character counts words do. This means you will be able to include additional information concerning your brand, which would have been impossible if you were using text.

Below are a few ways to utilize emojis in your bio:

- Try combining a few words with emojis. Feel free to be creative about this.

- Utilize emojis to draw attention to your content's key point. You can also utilize them as bullet points to separate texts and make them less difficult to read

- Any emojis you add to your bio should relate to what you do and should enhance your bio.

- Using emojis without any accompanying texts is not advisable. It may confuse your audience, and in doing this, you are just wasting space you could have used for something vital.

Also, note that you can be creative with your use of emojis. Toy with various emojis to determine the most suitable for your brand.

Website URL: Including A Link in Your Bio

Instagram only gives you the chance to include one clickable link, which comes up beneath your bio. Many Instagram users showcase the URL of their site's homepage, which is a smart move if you want to push more traffic to your website.

But, if your Instagram and your business objectives change along the line, you need to also change your URL link to support the new goal. You can include a link to your recent blog post or marketing campaign. There are a ton of options available for you to exploit here, so ensure you get the best from your link in your Instagram bio by letting it align with the objectives of your business.

CTA or Call to Action

An ideal location to include a call to action or CTA is your Instagram bio. Let your audience know the action you want them to take, and if you can, how to go about it.

For instance, request that they follow you on other platforms. If you have a product, you can also ask that they make a purchase. If you have a physical address for your business, you can include it in your bio alongside your opening and closing times, to ensure people can locate you and visit you with ease. Besides, you can request that your followers open a specific web page, by including the URL in the space allocated for a website.

Pick a Profile Image

This is the last step of the process. You need to pick a great profile picture, and the ideal choice is to go with your brand logo, which is already in use on your other social media platforms and website. When you use a symbol that is easy to identify, it will make it easier for your target audience to find you. It will also aid in elevating your brand awareness by ensuring it is visible on social media within your niche market.

A great Instagram brand bio consists of a range of components. However, you are allowed to be flexible and creative with this. Try numerous texts, calls to actions, and emojis. By frequently changing your Instagram bio, you will learn what triggers a response from your audience, and what functions for your organization.

The next step after ensuring your bio is as great as it can be, is to choose the right niche to focus on. We will be viewing how to go about this in the next chapter.

Chapter 4

Choosing the Right Niche

You have learned how to make posts of Instagram; you also understand why a name is vital. You have even created a great brand and bio, and so you begin to post random, high-quality content. You sit back and wait for the likes and comments to come in as your followers grow because you have done everything right.

However, you don't see any progress. Not many people aside from those you follow seem to have any interest in your posts. The issue may not be with what you are posting, but the way you post them. There is a range of individuals on Instagram using it effectively for their marketing needs. This is because they understand how the platform works and have learned to use it to their benefit for the best result.

One thing lots of marketers use to make themselves stand out is picking a niche and staying consistent with it. That way, they build themselves as authorities in that niche and are the first ones that come to the minds of users when they think of anything that relates to that niche. Knowing this, we will be covering everything about choosing a niche and making yourself stand out on Instagram in this chapter. But first, what is a niche?

What Is a Niche?

We may keep hammering on you choosing the right niche, but the truth is, if you don't know what a niche is, you won't even know where to begin.

A niche market is typically a part of a broader market. Similar to a slice of pizza. For instance, a market could be games, while niches within that consist of PS4 games, Xbox games, PC games, and so on. You can narrow it down a little further by saying PS4 sports games, Xbox adventure games, etc. When you define your niche market, it implies that you have a clear understanding of your target market and all the vital information, what they require, and how you can make it available for them.

Choosing a niche ensures it is less challenging to target, promote, and deliver. Why invest time marketing PS4 games to users who have a passion for Xbox games only? In addition to helping you target with ease, a niche can help you make lots of profit and save you the cash you would have used in marketing to the wrong audience. When choosing a niche market, you don't just pick the first subject that comes to mind, or you may never go far. There is a right way to choose a niche, which we will cover below.

How to Pick a Niche Market?

People should know your Instagram page for a specific thing. This may be any topic you have an interest in, which could range from mobile phones to footwear. Any niche you choose must be one you are passionate about and can make endless posts on without getting bored.

If you are having problems narrowing down your niche, you can search Instagram a bit deeper. Go through the best pages that have to do with subjects that interest you. Know the individuals in that field, and the hashtags that are typically used with that specific subject.

Choosing a niche for yourself should be less complicated the instant you know if the niche has a presence on Instagram or not. Now, the next step is to determine your audience.

Determine Your Audience

After deciding what you will be posting about, you need to determine the individuals you will be speaking to online. To resolve this, ask yourself these questions:

- Who are my customers or audience?

- What value can I offer with my interests?

- What kind of content will I have the capacity to offer?

- How much engagement do I want?

- How much traffic can I conveniently handle each month?

The reason for these questions is to determine your customers so you can structure your content to prove to them they have an interest in the same things you do. If people can relate to your posts, they will follow you with ease. If you are in the dog niche, you can focus your content on dog care, dog leashes, best dog breeds, tutorials, etc.

The value you provide your community is vital because it lets your followers know your posts are relevant, and it will help them decide if they will keep seeing your posts or ignore them. The instant users know that they can get the most recent and accurate information about their favorite niche; you will soon become an authority and have a consistent flow of audience.

Develop a Strategy

Now that you have determined your niche and your audience, the next thing to do is to develop a strategy. If you are beginning, it is ideal to pick a niche and remain in that niche to increase the number of followers you have. An easy way of doing this is to follow individuals who share some similarities with your account and have the same interests.

Also, you will want to leave witty comments on their posts anytime they drop something new. The more you engage with the community, the higher the possibility of you gaining followers from there too. With time, they will also engage with your posts by commenting, liking, or sharing them. This is the point your content becomes vital. You want to ensure your content is informative and supported by videos and pictures to prove that you are providing the community with value. With time, the number of followers you have will increase and perhaps feature on the pages of others. When you develop a good strategy, it gives you the chance to interact with other pages efficiently.

Remain Steady

The instant you have increased your follower count; you need to remain consistent with your posts. When you post is vital, but you need to remember that what you post is more critical. If you go a week without any posts, with time, your followers will begin to forget you. To determine how frequently you should post, you can take a look at similar pages and see what they do. If they post two times a week, you need to post four times. If they make posts every 3-4 days, it's best to make yours daily until you grow more prominent instead of mirroring what they do. Remain consistent and leave posts that are relevant to your audience.

Ensuring You Have a Profitable Niche

You need to understand that not all niches offer the same kind of returns. Although you want to pick something you have a passion for, you still need a niche that will bring you adequate returns. It is not impossible to pick a niche that is not narrow enough.

For a niche to be profitable, it requires adequate numbers. To determine this, ask yourself the following:

- Are there sufficient individuals who have an interest in it to amass revenue consistently?

- Are people keen on spending their funds in the niche?

- Will you be able to provide a solution to a need, want, or problem for them?

- Can you enhance on a currently existing solution?

If your response to these questions is yes, then your niche is a profitable one. Nonetheless, you can try out other niches, mainly if you aim to make a profit in the long run. That being said, below are some of the most profitable niches you can choose on Instagram.

Profitable Niches on Instagram

There are a lot of niches that become popular for a while and phase out. Taking advantage of what is presently in vogue is not a terrible idea, but you never can tell when it will vanish. A better option is to find a subject in markets that are always profitable.

These are niches, or markets that are will always remain fresh, trendy, and popular years down the road. Below are a few of these niches:

Health and Fitness

Health and fitness services, products, content, and tools will always be in high demand. Most individuals take their health seriously, be it emotional, mental, physical, or otherwise to a reasonable extent.

You can provide hacks, tricks, or tips for people to stay healthy. You can also share your journey to wellness, fitness, or health. Also, you can suggest services and products which you produced or that of others. There is always a broad audience in the health and fitness niche, and they can never get enough. A few of the most recognized niches in this market include weightlifting, basketball, football, yoga, and cycling, among others.

Travel

Many of us imagine ourselves taking adventures in luxury locations. There is often a particular country or area we would love to check-out. In 2017, the travel industry had a value of $5.29 trillion, which makes it a very viable sector to tap into ("How much is the travel industry worth? Try US $5.29 trillion - Travelweek", 2019).

However, because this is a prevalent market, you need to narrow down your niche to the fullest if you want to have an effect on the market. Suggest and review locations to eat, places to stay, various cities, ways to move around in specific cities and fantastic videos and pictures for individuals in niches for outdoor enthusiasts, business travelers, and backpackers among others.

Beauty

The beauty market audience consists of mostly women, but there are also men that find it appealing, and it is not fading away any time soon. It has been estimated that by 2024, the cosmetics industry will get to $863 billion ("Global Cosmetic Products Market Will Reach USD 863 Billion by 2024: Zion Market Research", 2019).

The #Beauty has more than 200 million posts associated with it, and the number is growing continuously. Sharing product reviews, tutorials, and how-to's is a great way to begin. And because beauty has a lot to do with visuals, it is a perfect fit for Instagram, which has 50.3 percent, female users ("Global Instagram user age & gender distribution 2019 | Statistic", 2019). A few of the top niches in the beauty market include makeup, skincare, hair, and nails.

Business

Money is essential for almost every individual. If you are well-versed in things that have to do with business, then tapping into the business niche is a great way to go. Perhaps you are a business coach who offers services that are vital to business owners like PR or marketing, or a business consultant who aids owners of businesses.

With numerous business owners presently on Instagram, this is undoubtedly a niche you will want to take advantage of. As usual, you need to focus, so don't try to generalize your niche. Rather, narrow it down and do it well. Offer tricks, how-to's, and hacks which lots of individuals will find useful; and with time your followers will grow, filled with individuals who would be willing to patronize you when you have something to sell.

Some of the most popular niches in this market include blogging, marketing, real estate, starting a business, and eCommerce, among others.

Fashion

This is a spin-off from the beauty market, however, it is a massive market on its own. Consider what is distinct about your style, then create a business along with a page on Instagram that portrays this style. Creating content will be very easy, considering you are just being yourself.

Also, it is not essential for you to be a professional fashion designer to tap into the fashion niche. Perhaps you understand how to develop the ideal look each day, or you have a still that is so distinct and appealing you turn heads anywhere you go. If your contact is unique and authentic, you will grab the attention of people quickly.

The following include some of the leading niches you can tap from in the fashion market: accessories, clothing, watches, and jewelry.

Lifestyle and Luxury

Everyone loves the good life and wishes to have a taste of it. If you enjoy taking pictures of cars, food, or your daily life, then this niche may be just what you need. The lifestyle niche has to do with you offering a look into the life that lots of people desire, regardless of if it is a life filled with positivity or that of a professional in a specific field.

The luxury niche, on the other hand, has to do with showing a glimpse of the life we all dream of. Notwithstanding the one you choose to go with, they are both very profitable and well-recognized. Some of the niches here include supercars, travel, and houses, among others.

Animals

In 2017, the pet sector amassed $86 billion in the United States (Schmidt, 2018). It has also been projected that pet care will surpass a worldwide estimate of $202 billion in the coming years ("Pet Care Market Size Worth $202.6 Billion By 2025 | CAGR: 4.9%", 2018). These include food, toys, pet insurance, treats, and clothing among a host of others.

Lots of men and women alike have a deep-rooted passion for animals and treat them like family. Tap into this love and enjoy the possibilities that come with it.

Relationships

There will always be relationship issues and drama in this world because everyone has them. For this reason, the relationship niche is a great one to exploit. Individuals are always in search of ways to understand the opposite sex, enhance their relationship among others. This means in this niche; you can gain a reasonable amount of following fast.

A few specific niches you can tap from in this market include parenting, business relationships, and friends. If you have tutorials and tips that can make it easy for people in relationships, then there is a lot of revenue to be made.

Gaming

Games are appealing to kids and even lots of adults. If you are close to someone who loves games, you most likely have an idea of how much games can be worth.

Individuals spend lots of money purchasing consoles, games, walkthroughs, and guides. Some of them even enjoy watching others review and play the most recent and expected games on YouTube and other platforms.

There are individuals on Instagram that make tons of cash playing and reviewing video games as a full-time job. One of these is the recognized PewDiePie who has more than 14 million followers on Instagram. This niche is quite broad and still offers a lot of possibilities to newcomers.

Family/Parenting

This is another spin-off from the relationship market, but then this is a niche which is rising tremendously. Let's face it, being a parent is not easy and all new parents are always in search of advice to ensure they take all the right steps. Some want advice on products to purchase to make things easier. In 2018, the industry for baby care product was worth $73.86 billion (Johnson, 2019). Accounts focused on this niche appeal to lots of individuals because they can relate to it. Even if you have no kids, you indeed came from a family which makes it one of the more profitable niches you can find out there.

By now, you should have decided on your ideal niche. But even with the right niche, learning how to post high-quality content is still vital, or you won't get the kind of engagement you desire. The chapter below will delve deeper into this.

Chapter 5

Developing High-quality content

on Instagram

For many individuals, creating content of high-quality can be a difficult task. Developing ideas and locating the appropriate visuals for your feed is easier in theory. In addition to being exciting and significant to your target audience, your content also has to look amazing.

Also, Instagram is a platform which is incredibly visual, and effective marketing campaigns rely heavily on engaging and appealing images. All of these combined increases the pressure to search for great content.

However, it does not have to be so tedious to create quality content on your Instagram account. There are a lot of techniques to use in creating high-quality content, and we will be taking an elaborate look at them in this chapter. But first, why do you need quality content on Instagram?

Benefits of High-Quality Content

To develop brand credibility and your target audience, you need to consistently make your content distinct. Before you advertise products or set up shoppable feeds, your content is what draws in the audience and transforms them into followers. Having quality content comes with a lot of benefits which include;

It Helps in Building Brand Loyalty

When it comes to the competitive field of social media, you only get one opportunity to make yourself stand out. With quality content, you can build trust and loyalty. A good way of attaining success on Instagram is to utilize the 80/20 rule. Offering value should be 80 percent of the time, while promotion should stay at 20percent.

Enhance Rate of Conversion

Contests, User-generated content, rewards, and CTs are types of contents that have a considerable possibility of enhancing your rates of conversions on Instagram. You can exploit all the opportunities offered by Instagram. For instance, even though hyperlinks are not allowed anywhere outside your bio, you can still take advantage of a CTA to urge your followers to take targeted action and transform them into prospective clients. Knowing these benefits, how then do you create high-quality content on Instagram? You will be learning this in the next section.

How to Develop High-Quality Content

As we have previously covered, Instagram is a social media channel which is based on visuals. This means the content you require to keep your audience engaged on Instagram has to do with Stories, videos, and photos. Before you make any post, the first step is to determine your objective.

What do you plan on accomplishing with your content? The following could be examples of some of your objectives:

- To promote an existing or new product

- To increase awareness for your business page or get more followers

- To draw in traffic to your website from your Instagram page

The instant you have put your objectives in place, the next thing you need to do is develop engaging content. Below are a few procedures to help you begin:

Find Out More about Your Audience

If you develop any content without knowing your audience, you may end up with the wrong kind of content. To learn about your audience, you need to determine the following:

- How do they utilize Instagram?

- What Instagram accounts do they have an interest in?

- Why are they on the platform?

To streamline things, you can carry out surveys or interviews with numerous individuals in your target group. This will help you determine their areas of needs and learn what is vital to them.

Think about Content with the Best Performance

Instagram has to do with images, but when it has to do with Instagram, you need to streamline your options. You need to share content that improves your visual presence and brings your brand utility to light.

You need to ensure you keep a narrative outline in all your images, so it can be easy to recognize you going forward. So what are the kinds of content you can share on Instagram? Below are some of your options:

- Share the beliefs and values of your organization

- Post pictures of your workplace. Give your followers the chance to create a connection with you and not only your service or product.

- Share Pictures of Individuals Utilizing Your Products

Even if you post the right kinds of content, if they do not align, then it may be challenging to succeed. This is why you need to develop patterns and themes for your content.

Develop Content Patterns and Themes

Having reviewed the expectations of your audience and what your goals are, you need to choose components of your brand, which you can emphasize via your Instagram content. Your services, team members, and brand products are all great places to begin for content themes. Next, think of topics that align with your stories, photos, and videos, and ensure the themes of your content go with your visuals. Even with a great theme, having poorly edited images or using random filters can affect the overall outcome of your content. This is why you need to learn to use filters the right way.

Learn to Use Filters

As stated by Canva (n.d.), the most utilized filter on Instagram is Clarendon. With this filter, you can highlight your images, brighten them, and also add shadows to make them appealing. Use a constant filter that tallies with the persona of your brand and offers it a consistent and distinct look.

According to a study carried out by Yahoo Labs and Georgia Tech, utilizing filters and including amazing copies to pictures could help enhance viewability by as much as 21 percent. It can also lead to a 45 percent enhancement in the number of comments (Friedman, 2015).

Exploit Hashtags

The main perks of hashtags is their capacity to ensure your content is more discoverable. In return, it grows your post engagement and audience. When categorizing content, Instagram capitalizes on hashtags. A good approach is to utilize them for the keywords you include in your copies.

To get the best from your content, you can try incorporating branded hashtags into each post. In doing so, you can link them to your brand, and oversee them with the aid of a tool for social media listening. There is no right amount when it comes to the number of hashtags you will be able to include in captions. However, it is vital to remain relevant and add hashtags that have to do with anything you post on Instagram. It is not ideal to fill your posts with irrelevant hashtags, all because you want more. Doing this can have a negative impact instead of the positive one you desire.

Pay attention to UGC Content

UGC means User Generated Content. It is a very efficient technique for raising your brand awareness on Instagram. UGC is when individuals who use a specific brand distribute its content with or without the brand motivating them.

If your brand is well-established and trusted, this approach would work well for you. But, if you are still making efforts to find a place for your brand online, no user will develop content regarding your brand without any encouragement or reward. For this reason, you need to run a promotional event or a contest where users would get a reward if they create and share content on your brand's behalf.

Cash in On Captions

Great visuals are a significant part of Instagram; however, it is also vital to have a productive caption. The reason is that it enhances comments and likes on your posts, and also drives engagement.

Instagram states that posts displayed in user feeds are presented based on the potential interest of the user in the content being offered. In simple terms, it implies that contents with a vast amount of comments and likes are better candidates to be presented at the top of the feed of your followers.

Instagram captions have the function of showcasing your brand's personality, entertaining your audience, and urging followers to take action. With captions, you can tell a moving story that will serve the final objective of your brand. There is no particular method of creating captions that work for everyone. Instead, the best option is for you to find what works for you.

Taking the captions on Nike's Instagram page, for example; some of their posts aim to inspire the audience while some are motivational. Take a cue from this and find out what works for you.

Repost Content from Brands Similar to Yours

What if you don't have the time to develop quality content for yourself? The great news is that it is not essential. If you are in a viable niche, there is a high possibility that there are other accounts consistently developing content that piques the interest of your audience.

It is not a bad idea to post content from Instagram bands that are similar to yours, or accounts that are significant to your Instagram strategy and followers, so long as you request authorization and appropriately credit the source.

To repost Instagram content, the right way, this what you have to do:

Follow Accounts and Hashtags to Find Content of High-Quality

To find the content you can repost, think of brands that have exhilarating Instagram accounts, which are not in direct competition with you, and have an audience similar to yours.

Take a look at their accounts and note the ones that create the leading contents you can share. Follow them so you can be notified about their new posts and save any particular posts you feel you can share on your page. You can easily do this by using the bookmark icon, which you can find underneath any video or post on Instagram. Better still, you can save the posts you plan on re-posting in a separate collection.

Another great way is to follow hashtags that are significant to your account. The excellent part of following hashtags is that posts linked to the hashtags you follow show up in your feed. This ensures it is less complicated for you to find fantastic content to repost. All you need to do is run a search for the hashtag on Instagram and follow!

Work with Influencers

If you want to get a continuous supply of quality content, working with influencers is a great way to go. This is because of their reasonable followers count. However, influencers are expensive, and if you have a limited budget, you can try working with a micro-influencer before you move to more recognized ones. When you collaborate with other micro-influencers in your niche, you will be able to reach around 10,000 to 40,000 individuals. This can be very significant if you work with influencers in the same niche as you. To contact influencers, you can send a DM or get their contact information from their bios.

Apps That Can Help You with Posting Content

As you must be aware, it can seem like a huge task to post content continuously. On average, many leading brands posts almost five times every week, which can consume numerous hours with ease. This is the reason lots of social media managers capitalize on applications that give them the capacity to load multiple contents and automate posting. Below are a few of the best apps that can help with posting and publishing content on Instagram.

Later

This is a platform established particularly for Instagram. This tool lets you schedule posts, monitor hashtags, and amass user-generated content among many others. Also, this app is an official partner of Instagram and utilizes their API for the importation of images, which makes it a very secure choice for organizations that are bothered about the safety of their social accounts.

Later does not cost anything for individuals, but you may need to pay some fees if you have a large company.

Buffer

Buffer is a scheduling application for social media, which is free of charge. You can integrate it with Instagram and a host of other recognized platforms on social media. With this application, you can post single images, and it also sends you reminders, to enable you posts videos manually and posts consisting of multiple images. This application is free for individuals but can be quite pricey for large brands with numerous users and accounts. Buffer comes as an iOS, web, and Android app.

Sprout Social

With Sprout Social, you can schedule posts on Instagram, manage comments, monitor hashtags, and run reporting. With this tool, you can schedule posts and automatically send them to Instagram. You can find this application online as a web app, Android, and iOS mobile application.

Hootsuite

Hootsuite is a very recognized platform for social media management. You can integrate it with all the core social networks apart from Instagram. With this application, you can automate posts and send reminders for posts. It is not as expensive as the competition, and you can use it as an iOS, Android, or web application.

Even if you develop the best content, posting it at the wrong time may not get you the traffic you want. You need to learn the right posting time for your content. We will be probing this more in the chapter to follow.

Chapter 6

Right Posting Time to Generate

Buyers

Even when you upload the best content on your Instagram page, if you are posting at the wrong time on Instagram, you are setting yourself up to fail. The time you post on Instagram is just as crucial as the quality of content.

However, all brands may not have the same ideal posting time. Although there are studies which state that there are specific periods of the day that are typically better for posting, this practice may not suit your brand. It is a great place to start, but you will still have to try what works for you by using various posting times to determine the ideal one for your followers and your brand.

Similar to other social platforms, Instagram takes advantage of a continuously changing algorithm that makes things a little harder. If you have determined the best time for posting your contents, you still have to stay ahead of the changes to these algorithms by experimenting on, measuring, and improving your techniques. The Instagram algorithm takes note of the level of engagements attained by your post and how fast users interact with them, so you need to locate the ideal time to enhance your reach.

What Is the Ideal Time to Post On Instagram?

This differs based on the day of the week, audience, and your time zone. For instance, a college students demographic will have a lot more time to spend on Instagram during the week as opposed to a business audience which will be working and not have as much time to invest in Instagram.

This is the reason you need to determine your best time to post, which we will be covering later in this chapter. Nonetheless, there are a few days during the week and weekends, which are consistent and ideal for all brands:

- 7 – 9 am – When most people head to work

- 12 – 2 pm – Lunch breaks

- 5 – 6 pm – Close of work

- 9 -11 pm – Bedtime scrolling

As stated by research done by ShareThis, most users tend to visit Instagram during their daily commute to work. Other peak periods for Instagram activities, also include lunch break and after work hours ("The Best Time to Post on Instagram By Day, Niche & More", 2019).

Average Ideal Time to Post During the Weekend (Saturday and Sunday)

- 9 – 11 am

- 2 – 5 pm

Weekend hangovers and brunches imply that users usually pick up their phones later in the morning. Another period of high engagement is during the mid-afternoon. Since weekends are typically work-free days, the ideal time to post differs based on your audience. Note that lots of individuals go out to have fun on Saturday nights, and so depending on your target market, it may be best not to make posts late Saturday nights. According to research by HubSpot, Instagram engagement on

Sunday is not great either, so it's best not to include it in your posting schedule (Chi, 2019).

Why Are These the Best Times to Post?

If you put your schedule into consideration, you will observe that your routine does not stay the same each day. These changes can have an impact on how and when you head onto social media channels.

Lots of active users on social media, go through their phones when they get up during a work week. Monday mornings are usually more tedious, so posting early Tuesday morning through Friday has tends to generate more engagement.

Also, many individuals find lunch hours to be a suitable time to head to social media. The afternoon is another period with a peak level of engagement because the mental energy of many individuals begins to wear off during this period, and social networking can offer them the much-needed break.

Saturday mornings are also peak periods that have tons of traffic on Instagram. Regardless of the activities, they are engaged in, these early hours during the weekend draw in a tremendous amount of traffic to the platform, which ensures people tend to view your content.

Determine Your Best Posting Time by Studying Your Industry Trend

Even though these general times for posting are great, to begin with, it is vital to determine your brand strategy, to enable you to target your precise audience with content relevant to them.

Sectors like tourism, technology, education, entertainment, and healthcare, do not have the same peak times. If your goal is to get to your target audience in your sector, you need to search for significant data to help you make the appropriate decisions. In doing so, you can determine the ideal time to upload your posts on Instagram.

How Does Instagram Algorithm Impact your views?

When pondering on the best posting time for Instagram, you need to learn how Instagram's algorithm has an impact on what users see. It emphasizes on recent posts, so newly uploaded posts have a higher tendency of showing up on the feeds of your users.

This algorithm influences when and if your target users will come across your posts. What this means is that you should endeavor to make your posts recent at the time your audience tends to visit Instagram.

The Instagram algorithm also analyses how much engagement a post gets when deliberating on whether to show it to your audience or not. The higher the comments, likes, and shares, the more Instagram will let your posts show up in the feeds of your audience. If you can post during peak hours, you will encourage engagement and aid each post in getting to much more of your audience.

Are Time Zones Vital?

If your core audience is situated in a precise area, like the East Coast, be certain to utilize the recommended times of their time zone. The same applies if your audience is made up of individuals who do not reside in the United States. You need to consider their time zone. You can still use the guide above even if your followers have numerous time zones.

For instance, you could upload your post to Instagram at the typical time for waking up, plan another post for mid-day, and schedule an additional post for late in the afternoon for the time zone you are targeting. If your audience is spread within numerous time zone, you can let some posts perform dual roles at once. This means they can be as a commute post in a specific time zone and after work post in another.

This may seem a little complex, but there is a range of tools that can help you with this. Instagram comes with in-built tools that can be of help, while third-party applications like Later are also at your disposal.

How to Determine the Peak Periods of Your Audience?

If your Instagram account is for business, you can take advantage of the Instagram insights tool to examine the demographics of your followers, activity, and engagement trends. This very efficient tool for analytics can aid you in making informed decisions regarding the most appropriate time for your specific audience.

You can find the data of your custom-made Instagram insights by heading to your account page via your Instagram application. Close to the top of your screen, you will find a bar graph icon –hit this, and you will find important data about how individual stories and posts are performing. You will also learn about comments, impressions, and the number of individuals that have followed and unfollowed you. With these insights, you will be able to learn the kind of content that reverberates with your audience. You will also be able to evaluate how successful your campaigns have been.

Additionally, the Followers area of Instagram insights offers you vital data about the most active period of your audience on the platform. You will be able to access a graph that lets you see the period of each day the individuals who follow you are most active and an additional graph that shows the days your followers come online. With this information, you will be able to determine activity patterns for your core audiences. Having knowledge of the times and days of peak usage will help your efforts in targeted posting.

It is vital for you to closely monitor your Instagram insight trends. However, the peak activity times of your audience will most likely change as they grow, so you need to adjust when you observe a change in the peak engagement periods. You don't want to miss the chance to connect with your audience as it develops and goes through change.

How Frequently Should You Post on Instagram?

Making frequent posts is vital to growing your following and ensuring your content gets on the feed of your audience. If you want your Instagram feed to continue being engaging and lively, you can get inspiration from established brands. According to research, leading companies upload Instagram contents 1.5 times on average each day.

How can you tap from this? Strive to upload posts one to two times each day. And the instant you have determined a posting rhythm, it is vital that you remain consistent. Imagine the effect on your account, if you made a post daily for many weeks, then reduce it suddenly to one or three times each week. Your audience may not have as much interest, and you may experience a reduction in your engagement.

To avoid this issue, it is ideal for you to begin at a slower speed. If you can manage two times a week for a start, go from there and make plans to develop with time. Ensure your focus is on quality and not quantity. You will get a higher level of engagement by uploading amazing photos accompanied by great captions, in contrast to filling your account with substandard content.

As you understand your scheduling tool and get more comfortable with looking for content and creating it, you can increase your post frequency. The instant you have developed a regular rhythm of amazing content; your audience will be glad when you start to post more frequently.

Scheduling Posts: Why Is It Essential?

To maintain engagement and relevance on Instagram, you have to put in a lot of effort and some investigation. However, it is not compulsory to stay behind your account all day, to get to your audience. Rather, you can take advantage of scheduling tools like Later and Hootsuite.

A majority of these tools for scheduling are easy to use. And although some of them emphasize solely on scheduling, others come with in-built features for analyzing the audience. With these features, you will be able to get more insight into the engagement and activity of your audience. You will also get suggestions for the ideal posting periods tailored to your precise audience.

This can reduce the amount of manual analysis you will have to carry out, letting you pay attention to developing content of high quality with a great audience appeal. It will also inform you of the ideal time to upload posts on Instagram to ensure you satisfy your followers.

When you schedule your posts on Instagram, you will have the capacity to make your marketing efforts more efficient. Rather than posting every day, you can plan posts. Sometimes, this could be weeks or months ahead. It lets you keep an active presence on social media with much less effort. Additionally, if you develop great content, you can plan them to fall at peak periods for the broadest viewership possible.

Another benefit if using schedule tools is how you can repurpose content with ease. You will have the capacity to take a post that thrived on Instagram and share it other platforms like YouTube, LinkedIn, Facebook, and others. Better still, you can develop multi-layered campaigns, which can encourage your audience to perform a specific action, like signing up for your newsletter and attending webinars.

Understanding the ideal time to make posts on Instagram can help you generate real buyers. It is also a way of developing a successful Instagram presence. You can utilize this knowledge to offer content to the appropriate followers when the time is right, and before you know it, your follower base will grow even more.

Chapter 7

Ways to Make Money On

Instagram

Instagram is a platform for sharing your passion using short videos and pictures. It also allows you to connect with individuals who share similar interests with you, develop loyal followers, and become a top influencer in your specified niche. Now, lots of accounts on Instagram have tons of followers.

Typically, many brands have noticed the room for advertising the influence and reach of these accounts can create. For this reason, users with a decent amount of followers now have numerous ways to make money using the platform. That being said, this chapter will cover the various methods you can use in earning money on Instagram. But before we delve into that, let's take a look at some of the essential things that have to be in place.

What Do You Need to Earn Cash Via Instagram?

The leverage of an Instagram user stems from the numbers of followers he/she has. The reason is that Instagram profiles that have numerous followers offer connection to a massive market. If you are serious about earning money on Instagram, you need to begin small and take all the chances possible to enhance the follower count on your account. Now, let's go into this a little further.

Influence and Reach

The natural growth of your followers has a direct relationship with the level of reach your posts have. You have numerous options to expand your posts reach, but one that is important for making cash off Instagram are authentic and original posts. You will need to have no less than three thousand followers on your profile before it becomes lucrative. This means you need to invest the time to amass followers who find you trustworthy, and who believe your posts have something significant to offer them.

If you aim to use your Instagram profile in promoting the products and services of organizations, then you need more than good reach. This is because people still have to make a move and buy the product or service you are promoting. The capacity to coax your followers into purchasing the products or services you are providing is known as influence, and if you plan on becoming a leading influencer on Instagram, you have to learn the skill of persuasion.

Even if your Instagram follower count is not a hundred thousand, there may be organizations who will be intrigued by your profile and would be keen on offering you a sponsorship if your social media presence is powerful enough to induce others to take the desired action. The level of communication you have with your followers is also as vital as your influence. If your followers don't interact with your posts, they will hardly take action.

Engaged Followers

If you are not getting comments or likes from those who follow your page, then it means your posts are not significant enough to keep them engaged and trigger a response from them. In contrast to this, if your posts are drawing in lots of likes and comments, it means the posts are helping your Instagram followers solve a specific issue they may be facing.

Also, the number of messages your Instagram followers send to you is something you should consider in determining how engaged your followers are with your posts and pages. For this reason, it is crucial that you have people continuously leaving comments on your posts, sharing them, liking them, and tagging their followers in your posts, if you are serious about sparking interest in profiles and brands that can help you make money on Instagram.

Like we covered earlier, if your posts are unable to trigger any form of response from your followers, then the number of followers won't matter. This is why you have to search for ways to enhance the number of comments and likes you get on your posts if you aim to make money on Instagram.

Now that you understand the necessary requirements, let us move on to the best ways to make money via Instagram.

Ways to Earn Money on Instagram

There are numerous ways of earning cash available at your disposal. Below are a few of the top options:

Become an Influencer

Like we have covered above, being an influencer means you can influence your followers, and control the way they feel about products and trends. This will be due to your position and the trust you have developed with your online image.

You can choose to partner with organizations as an influencer, to promote the services and products they offer. Lots of brands are eager to work with influencers to advertise their services and products. This is typically done via sponsored posts because of the numerous benefits of advertising on Instagram offers.

A sponsored post is one which displays a brand, service, or product which comes alongside branded hashtags, captions and URLs for whatever is being advertised. As an influencer, you can earn cash if you share these sponsored posts. Many companies are investing a lot of money in online advertising campaigns, and a decent portion goes to the leading influencers for every sponsored post published on their Instagram pages.

To do this effectively, you have to pick a niche that aligns with your image and lifestyle, have a specific audience, and develop authentic and relevant content. Many sponsors may even make the first contact with you if you have a decent number of followers. If you are having issues locating sponsors, there are numerous communities online you can become a member of to ensure it is less challenging to identify sponsors. A few of these include ***iFluenze***, ***Heartbeat***, and ***TapInfluence***, among a host of others.

Use Instagram to Sell Your Photos

Instagram's core focus is on visual content. For this reason, authentic photos of high quality will help you draw in numerous buyers. These consist of pictures, videos, simple art drawings, selfies, painting, and other kinds of visual content.

If you joined Instagram because of your skill in taking photographs, there are numerous platforms where you can sell your stock pictures. You can also advertise your photos and images on Instagram using marketplaces like ***Foap Community***, and ***Twenty20***, among others.

In essence, if you enjoy taking pictures, this is a fantastic way of selling your work and earning cash via Instagram. Upload your images and add hashtags, captions, a personalized watermark to prevent against theft, and include the photo details to draw in prospective buyers. Take a look around the marketplace to determine the most suitable method for you.

Selling pictures is not limited to experienced photographers alone, as if you can study how to use various editing tools to create professional images; you might have a gold mine on your hands.

Become an Affiliate Marketer

Affiliate marketing shares some similarities with influencer marketing, but then there is a major difference; affiliate marketers lay emphasis on making actual sales for a commission on every sale as opposed to Influencers that help in creating awareness about a brand or product. This means if you choose to become an affiliate marketer, you are offered a commission for each product you sell.

Being an affiliate is very simple. First, you get a unique URL, which is utilized by the affiliate program in tracking the number of individuals who click on the link and make a purchase from the website. This is the way you attain your commission. These promo codes or links take users directly to the page for purchasing the product. However, Instagram does not support the placing of clickable links in any location apart from your bio, which makes it challenging to use links. For this reason, Promo codes are the best routes for affiliates as you can integrate them into your Instagram stories and posts. With this, prospective customers will only have to input your promo code when they are about checking out, for you to attain your commission, while a discount is also offered to the customer on the product.

The Unique links for promoting affiliate offers are usually quite lengthy, so you may want to use a URL Shortener to make it shorter and more customer friendly. There are numerous affiliate programs you could sign up for to begin. You can check out the range of online communities to locate the ideal affiliate program for you. Some of these communities include ***Amazon's Affiliate Program***, and ***ClickBank*** among a host of others.

Trade Your Instagram Account

Many individuals deal in exchanging Instagram accounts for funds. This may be because they no longer have an interest in using Instagram for that moment, or they have a lot of accounts with decent follower counts and are interested in making cash.

Platforms like ***Viral Accounts*** and ***Fame Swap*** are popular places to sell your Instagram accounts. Depending on the platform you choose to go with, the rates may differ, and you can do your research to find the price suitable for you and dispose of your account for a reasonable sum of cash. However, you need to think critically about this, because you never can tell when your account may be of use to you later. Before you sell-off, your account, make sure your mind has been made up.

Sell Products on Instagram

It is possible to use your Instagram profile to sell products, be it an online service, or a digital or physical product. If you have good reach on your account and you have developed awareness for the product, all that is left is for you to promote your company and watch people troop in to buy your goods or services.

Instagram has offered a very budget-friendly and easy means to buy and sell, and using this factor is quite easy. All you need to do is establish a great brand name, and when you have developed a specific level of trust, people may even begin to do your marketing for you.

A lot of entrepreneurs began their businesses from Instagram, and many of them are at the top of their fields and enjoying a continuous influx of revenue. The great news is that; there is enough space for everyone to benefit from this as well. So if you have a product to sell, Instagram may be an excellent platform to start.

Get More Website Traffic Using Instagram

If you run a business which has a website, Instagram can offer a great platform to market that business. Raise awareness for your business and upload amazing images and content that can provide your business a distinct identity, then utilize than in drawing in visitors to your site.

If your audience finds your content engaging and relevant, they will want to learn more about your organization. To make this work, you need to add a link to your website on your bio, and visitors will be directed to your website from there. In turn, this will aid in increasing your product and service awareness, and with time, your conversion.

Another excellent method of staying on top of this is to provide offers and discounts, because using exclusive offers to market your services aside from boosting your conversion, also does the same to your number of followers. This is because they will be able to locate offers that are not available in other locations. The implication of all of these is the complete growth of your business, but ensure you add a link to your website, as without it, you won't get the traffic that will help increase sales.

Drop shipping to Users on Instagram

As a drop shipper, it means you run a business without the need for a physical store. All you require is a dealer who can convey your merchandise straight from their storeroom to your clients, which eradicates having to hold expensive product inventory. You also don't have to deal with the process of shipping, and you function as your own agent.

The concept is similar to selling products; however, in this situation, you don't have to store any product of goods, which makes it seamless for entrepreneurs and owners of businesses.

There are numerous e-commerce channels like the well-recognized ones like **_Oberlo_** and **_Shopify_**, which allow you to start a drop shipping store. To begin, you have to spot an ideal niche, then try out the product market to help you determine what would sell better. If you are looking for a cheap way of becoming a business owner, then drop shipping is a fantastic option, as it doesn't require a massive sum of cash to begin selling. If you use drop shipping the right way on

Instagram, there is a possibility of earning a lot of money in the long run.

With Instagram, you are open to a broad avenue of potential e-commerce. You can take advantage of the large number of individuals that are presently making money using this platform. Making money on Instagram is utterly dependent on the techniques and strategies you utilize, and the great thing is that you can invest yourself in more than one channel and be successful in them all. Now, all that is left is for you to head out and earn money via the Instagram platform. However, even if you understand how to make money on Instagram, if you don't know how to promote your services or the products you sell, nobody may even approach you in the first place. The next chapter will be digging into how you can exploit Instagram ads.

Chapter 8

Taking Advantage of Instagram

Ads

Instagram gets over one billion visitors each month. In addition to this, the numbers of engagement for this application is way more than Twitter and Facebook combined. This means you are losing out big time if you are not taking advantage of what the app has to offer.

This is the reason why this chapter will be teaching you how Instagram advertising works, and all the vital information regarding Instagram ads, so you can get your content across to the individuals on Instagram who matter to you. But first, we will be looking into what Instagram ad is.

Instagram Ads – What Is It?

Limited ad services were first introduced by Instagram when Facebook took over ownership in 2013. However, it only began to provide advertising access to various sizes of businesses and brands in 2015. These brands soon realized that Instagram was of enormous benefit for businesses.

Also, because Instagram is incorporated with Facebook Ads Manager, brands can take advantage of the enormous resources of user data Facebook offers, to advertise right to the audience they desire.

If you prefer numbers to understand how beneficial Instagram ads can be, below are a few statistics;

- Seventy-five percent of the Instagram users perform an action via Instagram ads like heading to a site or buying a product.

- Thirty-five percent of adults in America utilize Instagram("22+ Instagram Statistics That Matter to Marketers in 2019", 2019).

In essence, if you are not taking advantage of Instagram ads, you are depriving yourself of a considerable amount of possible revenue.

What Is the Cost of Instagram Ads?

Depending on your ad objectives, the cost may be unique to you. This is because all ads differ. However, for Instagram ads, the typical CPC (cost-per-click) is about $0.70 – $0.80. This figure was obtained from an evaluation of over $300million spent on ads. ("Instagram Ad Costs: The Complete Updated Resource for 2018", 2018)

Note that this is just like an estimate. You may end up spending more or less depending on numerous factors like the time of the year ads are set-up.

Creating Ads on Instagram

Now that you understand the basics, we will be taking a look at how to create ads. For this, we will be learning to do it using the Facebook Ad Manager, which is a prevalent method because it is easy to use. It also offers you the capacity to personalize your ad more than you would if you were using the application itself. Below are the steps that can help you create your ad.

Head to the Ad Manager via Facebook

Presuming you already have a Facebook account, and you are logged in, all you need to do is follow this link to get to the Facebook ad manager.

There is no precise Instagram Ad manager. You oversee Instagram ads via the Facebook Ads UI.

Determine Your Marketing Goals

Here, you need to pick a campaign goal. The great news is that the goals are clearly stated. If you are after additional traffic, select the traffic goal. If you want more engagement, choose the engagement goal, and so on.

However, there are only a few goals you can work with using Instagram ads, which include;

- Traffic

- Brand awareness

- Video Views

- Engagement: which works for just post engagement

- Conversions

- Reach

- App Installs

Determine your Target Audience

After determining your objective, you have to target the right audience, so your ad gets to the appropriate individuals. This is where Instagram ads flourish since you will be utilizing the demographic knowledge Facebook offers to get to the right individuals.

If you have previously utilized Facebook ads, you may have already built some audiences and understand the entire process. If you are using it for the first time, below are the targeting options you have at your disposal, which you can narrow down to reach a specific audience. For example, if you want to target men in Chicago, between the ages of 18- 25, who have an interest in sporting equipment, you will have the capacity to do that.

The targeting actions include;

- **Location**: lets you target a city, state, country, or zip code and ignore specific areas.

- **Gender**: Pick between all genders, or only men and vice versa

- **Age**: Lets you target different age ranges

- **Demographics**: You can access this under Detailed Targeting. It also has numerous sub-categories to pick from.

- **Languages**: Facebook suggests that you leave this place blank unless the language you want to target is not typical in the area you are aiming to target.

- **Behaviors**: This is also an option you will find under Detailed Targeting. It also provides you with numerous categories to check out. It could either be anniversaries, purchasing behaviors, job roles, and a host of other options.

- **Interests**: Still another option you will have access to under Detailed Targeting which offers numerous sub-categories to delve into. If you are in search of individuals who have an interest in horror movies, or beverages, you get these options and many more.

- **Custom Audience**: With this option, you will be able to upload your contact list and target leads or clients who you aim to upsell.

- **Lookalike Audience**: Here, Instagram gives you the chance to locate audiences who share lots of similarities to your other audiences.

- **Connections**: Here, you can target individuals connected to your app, page, or event.

After configuring your audience, Facebook also offers you a guide to how broad or specific your audience is. It is vital you take note of this because you want to choose a point where your audience is not too broad since it is not adequately targeted, but you don't want it to be too narrow either, since you may be unable to reach that many individuals.

Determine your Placements

The next step after targeting the demographic of your choice is to select your placement. This is vital if your campaign objectives are to show the ads on Instagram alone. If you decide to forgo this step, Facebook will let your ads show up on the two platforms.

This can be a positive thing, but if you have created content for Instagram, specifically, you need to pick the option "Edit Placements." From this point, you can choose Instagram as your placement, and if you would prefer the ads to show up on the stories or feed area of the platform. You also have the option of letting it show up on both.

Determine your Ad Schedule and Budget

If you understand how budgets work via AdWords, Facebook, and other platforms for running an ad, you may not have many issues with this step. If you have not, then it is not so much of a problem either, even though you may not understand how to put your lifetime or daily budget in place while running an Instagram campaign for the first time, you learn on the go. What's more, you also can pause or stop your ad at any point, if you believe your budget is not being apportioned the right way.

So which should you go with? A daily or lifetime budget? This is solely dependent on you, but if you decide to go with a daily budget, it ensures your budget does not get exhausted fast. In contrast, a lifetime budget gives you the capacity for scheduling your ad delivery. Both options do the work they should, so it is a matter of choice.

As mentioned earlier, you can schedule an ad to target certain moments of the week or day, that experience peak activity from your audience. If you are utilizing a lifetime budget, this can be an essential way of optimizing your budget.

Develop Your Instagram Ad

Here comes the moment you need to create your ad. Here, the set-up may seem different based on the objective you decide to go with.

There are six ad formats which Instagram provides you with. From the options provided, two show up on Instagram stories, while the other four show up on your Instagram feed. The latter is the option many marketers and advertisers take advantage of.

The options available include;

- Image Feed Ads

- Image Story Ads

- Video Feed Ads

- Video Story Ads

- Carousel Feed Ads

- Canvas Story ads

Every one of these ad formats is incorporated into the Stories and Feeds of the users which offer a non-distracting experience for users. Instagram also provides you a range of call-to-actions which can aid you in attaining more leads. We will be taking a look at each of them below:

Image Feed Ads

This is the most common ad format, and if you frequently use Instagram, there is a huge possibility that you may have come across it while perusing your feed. These ads consist of a single image which shows up when your target audience is going through their feed. The great thing about this ad is that if you do them properly, they will look like any other feed instead of ads.

Some of the specifications for this ad include:

- Type of file: Jpeg or PNG

- Max size of the file: 30MB

- Number of Hashtags: Maximum of 30

- Length of Text: 2,200 max. However, for the best delivery, Instagram suggests you stay below 90 characters.

Image Story Ads

This is similar to the Image feed ads, but they show up on the

Instagram Stories of your target.

The specifications include:

- 9:16 recommended image ratio and no less than 600 pixels' image width.

Video Feed Ads

You can give your ad more life using a video. If you create a video of high quality, then it is possible to promote it via your Instagram feed. Instagram offers support for various video files, but it is suggested that you use: square pixels, progressive scan, fixed frame rate, H.264 compression, and a 128kbps+ stereo AAC audio compression.

However, if you do have a video which fails to meet these requirements, numerous apps can aid you in altering your video.

Some of the specifications for video feed ads include:

- video resolution: No less than 1080 x 1080 pixels'

- Max file size: 4GB

- Max length of video: 60 seconds

- 125 characters' text length recommended

- Number of Hashtags: Maximum of 30

Video Story Ads

Stories are also great locations for running ads. This is because lots of users often expect to see videos here so it may not come as a surprise to see ads. The specifications for these ads are listed below:

- Video Resolution: No less than 1080 x 1920 pixels

- Video Length: Maximum of 15 seconds

- Maximum file size: 4GB

Carousel Feed Ads

Depending on how you use it, this format of ads can be quite fun. It lets you display a group of images users can scroll through instead of just one image. This kind of ad is ideal for brands that are very visual like those in the clothing industry, travel industry, food industry, and vehicle industry, among others.

You can use this to show your audience the faces behind your organization. The carousel feed ads let you include as much as ten images in one ad, all with a link to each product. Also, you have the option of adding a video to this form of ad.

The specifications for this ad include:

- Type of file: JPG or PNG

- Number of Hashtags: Maximum of 30

- Length of Text: 2,200 max. However, for the best delivery, Instagram suggests you stay below 90 characters.

- Max file size: 30MB

- Length of Video: Maximum of 60 seconds

Canvas Story Ads

Finally, the most recent inclusion to the ad formats, Canvas ads. With these ads, you can create a VR experience in your story. They only function on mobile devices and give you complete control of customization options. However, you need some technical knowledge. These ads can work alongside video, image, and carousel.

The specifications for this format are:

- Minimum width of the image: 400 pixels

- Max Height of Image: 150 pixels

Determining the Best Ad Format to Use On Instagram

Having understood the formats, you can choose from; you need to determine the best format for your needs.

You need to be deliberate about your ad format, and the question below can help you make a choice:

What Is Your Objective?

Your desired social media objective is the foundation for all the conclusions you make when it has to do with an ad campaign. It will aid you in determining what you should focus on and what you should not. Any ad you choose has to align with your objectives, always remember that.

Tips for Advertising On Instagram

Now that you understand the technical aspects of ad creation, below are a few things to note when developing an ad that will ensure engagement;

Know Your Audience

When you have an in-depth knowledge of your audience, you will be able to create messaging that they can connect with.

Before you begin to run any ads, you must have an intimate and in-depth knowledge of your audience.

Ask yourself:

- What solution does your service or product provide to them?

- What are their wants and needs?

- Do not forget their values and goals as you put your ads in place.

Utilize Texts Properly

Instagram does not let you use too many texts, but it does not have to be a negative thing. However, this means you need to offer the best value within the supported text character. While using your texts, ensure you are considering the personas of your audience.

Put engaging and appealing CTAs in place that will encourage your audience to perform any action you require.

Take Advantage of Hashtags

Many individuals tend to forget just how powerful hashtags can be. But if you learn to use them the right way, you will have an indispensable tool in your hands.

Including hashtags in Instagram posts enhances engagement by an average of 12.6 percent, which can make a whole lot of difference to your campaign. And if you take advantage of a branded hashtag, it can enhance awareness and engagement.

You have the capacity of utilizing as much as 30 hashtags on a single post. But don't get carried away; focus on the quality as opposed to the quantity.

Engage

You can group the interaction you have with social media users into two classes:

- Reactive Interaction: when you provide responses to mentions, direct messages, and comments on social media.

- Proactive Interaction: When you make the first contact with other users by engaging them. This can be very beneficial if you want to enhance the awareness around specific product launches or campaigns.

Ensure you do a bit of both as people engage and respond to your ads. It will help in developing your brand and ensure they understand you are not just another robotic organization.

Stay Consistent

Are you aware that more than 50 percent of the leading brands utilize a similar filter for each of their posts? ("33 Mind-Boggling Instagram Stats & Facts for 2018", 2019) The reason for this is simple: Consistency can aid in strengthening the image of your brand.

Every component of your brand should embody who you are as an organization. The tone, message, and visuals are all vital.

Regularly Switch Things Up

When you create a good ad, which seems to be doing so well and bringing you lots of engagement and traffic, it is easy to get attached. However, a great ad can only last for so long and may die down if you keep rinsing and repeating.

Change your ads as frequently as possible, so your audience doesn't get fed up with them. In addition to this, it will also help you understand the ads that offer you the best results. Try using various formats, captions, and audiences.

Measure Ad Performance

Using the Facebook Ads Manager, you can check out how your Instagram ads are performing. If you are using third party tools like Hootsuite Ads, you will be provided with a more comprehensive set of data that lets you view the best performing ads and those that are not working —and why they aren't.

In any strategy, monitoring performance and altering course when needed is very vital. But you also need to regularly check your Instagram analytics for a range of reasons which include:

- It can help you put in place realistic objectives and goals for every new campaign.

- It can help you monitor your competitors

Try Out Your Ad Copy

You need to try out various ad visuals and copy in a single campaign as it will also help things remain fresh.

Chapter 9

Targeting and Retargeting On Instagram

As a marketer, it can be quite infuriating to learn that prospective clients are slipping from your purchase funnel, for something that was not your fault. The internet offers a lot of distractions, and clients may check out your page, put a few products in their carts on your website, then they get distracted by something else and don't remember to make the final purchase.

The good news is that tracking these kinds of engagement and subtly pushing users to complete these actions is possible using Retargeting. In this chapter, we will learn what retargeting is and how you can include it in your marketing efforts. **What is Retargeting?**

In the digital space of today, retargeting is a very efficient method of converting leads. It is also known as remarketing, and it is a technique that has to do with taking previous leads –individuals who previously checked out your website, placed an item in their shopping cart or clicked an ad, and contacting them once more in a bid to convert them to final consumers.

They are ads which are structured in the form of reminders. The aim of retargeting is to help you make sales from the various existing audiences and leads you have. Retargeting offers a lot of potential to enhance your customer base, sales, and profits. This is because only around 2 percent of the primary web traffic leads to conversion the first time(Dunn, 2019). If you channel your resources into consistent and frequent retargeting efforts across all social media platforms, your possibilities are endless. If you are still not convinced about how retargeting can help your business, check out why retargeting is essential today.

Why Should You Retarget?

There are lots of individuals who may be skeptical of retargeting because it mainly has to do with keeping track of visitors. This can bring about some worries of privacy as many people have at some point gotten creeped out by continuous ads for an item we ran a search for in a store, months back.

If you do it the right way, retargeting does not have to bother anyone. If your tone and approach are strategic and authentic, you can be offering your audience an excellent service by jogging their memories about the presence of your brand. In the end, retargeting is one of the most efficient methods of offering viewers relevant ads built around their past behaviors and interests.

Aside from subtly nudging people to complete a purchase, you will also have the capacity to target your website visitors who checked out your tutorials or pricing pages. It will let you provide ads that directly satisfy their needs or interests. Also, with the growth of social media platforms which are driven by interest like Facebook, users have become familiar with the existence of interest-target ads, which makes remarketing something to expect.

Even though cookies and various tracking mechanisms have been around for a while, the process has been made easier for organizations to access due to the advent of Facebook's Pixel. When you incorporate Facebook Pixel to your site, you will have the capacity to participate in conversion tracking and build audiences based on views of a specific webpage.

Remarketing on a platform like Instagram, which many organizations and brands have not fully explored, can provide you with the capacity to locate new audiences on this incredibly visual platform. Furthermore, the integration of Facebook ads with Instagram also ensures it is less difficult to employ remarketing ads, which lead to high levels of conversions, thereby offering you more profit and a broader audience base. Now that you know why retargeting is something to take advantage of let's find out the steps to take for retargeting on Instagram.

Steps for Retargeting On Instagram

To accurately retarget on Instagram, the steps below can ensure you are successful

Install Facebook Pixel

The first thing you need to do is install the Facebook Pixel on your site. Pixel is an excellent tool for retargeting efforts. It is solely devoted to keeping track of all individuals that check out your website. With the data it offers, you will have a continuously increasing list of users, who are sure to know your product to some extent. If you don't know how to go about installing Facebook pixel on your site, you can offer the code to your site developer so they can get it done for you.

To ensure the pixel has been adequately integrated on your website, use the FB Pixel Helper, which is a plugin tool for Google Chrome, to find out.

Create the Audience You Want to Retarget

Next, you need to put a custom audience in place. These are the individuals you plan to send your ads to. Facebook gives you the chance to pick Website Traffic as the set of individuals to send ads to. This lets you draw in users who opened your website from the Custom Audience Pixel you have installed and lets them see your ads one more time.

To build your custom audience of individuals who have checked out your site in the past few days, all you have to do is head to your Facebook ads manager, then you select Tools – Audiences – Create Audience – Custom Audience – Website Customization. Then, pick your customization. When creating your audience, its best to choose those who visited your website during the past 180 days, as that is the highest option available.

Develop your Ad Campaign

Before you take this step, you have to hold on until people pay a visit to your website for the pixel to increase. See it this way; every visitor to your site with an account on Facebook is being lodged in a guest house, and when the guest house has enough lodgers, you can create your ad and target every individual in that guest house.

Depending on the level of traffic you get to your website, this may require only some minutes to a week. When you have adequate individuals in your audience, you will see "Ready" alongside a green dot.

If you have a reasonable amount of individuals in your "Retargeting Audience," you can then develop your ad campaign. To do this, create your Instagram ad campaign following the usual steps like we covered in Chapter 8.

Create Your Retargeting Ad Set

Here, you will determine the campaign's Ad set level. To start, set the schedule and designed budget you want the ad to run from. Next, pick the Custom Audience you created in the second step and set the ad's placement as Instagram. Next, make sure that there are individuals in your Audience by making sure your potential reach is more than 20.

If you are working with the typical Ads Manager, ensure only Instagram is selected and every other option is deselected if you want to use it for placement.

Create Your Retargeting Ad

Now you can create an ad that will be seen physically by your audience. Do not forget that people who have visited your website previously and have knowledge of who you are and what you do are categorized as "warm traffic" so you need to add some creativity to your ads.

Pick the appropriate Instagram and Facebook accounts and include the destination. Next, create an enticing ad that will lure your "warm traffic" to head back to your site and make a purchase or perform any other action you desire. If you want a more direct option for retargeting, try the Instagram dynamic ads.

Use Instagram Dynamic Ads for Targeting and Retargeting

Instagram Dynamic Ads was launched in 2016. It aids in advertising your products by letting people see ads that consist of products they previously showed an interest in —either by including it to their shopping carts or viewing it. The products shown to them could also be similar to what they purchased or displayed interest in.

On Facebook, more than 2 billion distinct items and products have been uploaded. Now, with Dynamic Ads being offered on Instagram, you can promote relevant merchandise to users who have checked your website across Instagram and Facebook.

This is the way to go if you want a straightforward method. You can automatically retarget the right individuals by showing them products they previously checked out. This is just another way for you to retarget via Instagram.

Takeaway

A poor retargeting strategy can be annoying from the client's perspective. This is the case where they continuously have to deal with ads from web pages they have no interest in.

However, Instagram comes in a design that gives your brand the chance to connect with audiences in a manner which is visual and not as intrusive as other platforms. There are retargeting campaigns that are properly created and targeted that viewers don't see as adverts but important reminders that direct them to make a purchase. This is the case with Airbnb's retargeting campaign.

When it comes to marketing on social media, regardless of the platform, the best strategy is to accept testing and repetition. Even if your brand has no plans to create a full-time campaign on Instagram, you can take advantage of the Facebook Pixel and get vital information to help you target the right users. Now is the time to retarget, with Facebook Pixel and its capacity to work on two of the leading platforms: Instagram and Facebook, it has never been any easier. Retargeting is a way of ensuring those who got to your page, buy your product. But how do you use Instagram to transform them into loyal customers in the first place? The next chapter will help you unravel this.

Chapter 10

How to Turn Your Audience Into

Customers

As a marketer or business owner, it is not entirely difficult to get new followers or audience. All you need to do as we have covered in earlier chapters is to stay consistent and share valuable content. However, when it comes to transforming the audience into paying customers, it is another story entirely, and you need to do more than post each day.

As stated by studies, 71% of individuals have a higher likelihood to purchase a product via recommendations from social media, while 74% get directions from social media when making purchase decisions ("How To Make An Impact On Consumers Mind | Lemonz Studios", 2018). What this means is that, when it comes to making decisions related to a purchase, customers are more devoted to social media.

As someone who provides or advertises products and services, it will only be to your benefit if you leverage this trend. Now, Instagram is the fastest rising social platform. In addition to being attractive and user-friendly to the younger generations, it also offers a barrage of benefits that can help your business make more sales. For this reason, you need to take all the necessary steps to transform your audience to life-long customers. This is what this chapter will elaborate on as we will be covering some techniques that can help you with this below.

Turning Your Audience into Customers

Below are a few tips that can help you transform your audience to life-long customers.

Do Some Research

As you begin to notice an increase in your followers count, take some time to learn what they have an interest in and who they are. What do they like? Are they professionals or students? Do they have a pending need? Are they your ideal clients?

Determining these is vital for a few reasons. First, when you know your followers, you can make your connection more personalized. Leave a comment on one of their posts. Doing this may not take more than a minute, but the effect to your customer can be of very high value.

Next, if you don't have an image of your perfect customer yet, it will help you start creating one. But, if you already have a clear picture, you can keep track of how properly you are drawing them in and help them meet their needs.

Provide Special Content

By providing exclusive content to your audience, you can further enhance the relationship you share with them. This will ensure they keep returning to you continuously and urges them to engage with your business on a personal level, and a long term basis.

The following are ways you can do this:

- Provide exclusive footage: Utilize Instagram to disclose products you have not shared on other platforms like Twitter or Facebook. Doing this will make your followers on Instagram feel special.

- Develop an exclusive offer: Provide a discount code to your Instagram followers, which you are letting them have.

- Launch an event or product via Instagram: Create a brief video of your organization taking a trip, or opening a new outlet.

Leverage Promotion

Promote a part of your business by establishing a social media giveaway which your fans will find exciting. This is vital because it helps your followers understand what you offer and what you do. It also helps in generating more engagement on your various pages on social media.

For instance, you can ask: "What is your best budgeting tip? The first respondent will be offered a free meeting with me on how to create a proper budget."

Structure Your Business or Store to Seem Amazing

One of the leading techniques you can use in transforming your audience into customers on Instagram is to create a business profile people would want to associate themselves with.

To do this, display pictures of your business place being a fun place to be. Imagine an image showing your co-workers having a team bonding weekend at the beach or a weekend barbecue. There are lots of ways you can spin this. Feel free to be creative here.

Another way to ensure your followers are more involved in your brand or company is to provide them with exclusive behind the scenes footage into the task you are working on.

A few ways to do this include:

- Show a picture of a product being sent to a customer

- Post an image of a meeting where your co-workers are busy speaking about a product.

- Show the before or after image of a meeting.

Be Loyal

To get loyal customers, you need to have loyal followers and fans. But if you want loyalty, you have to give allegiance.

And how is the best way to do this?

It is by staying consistent. Showing respect, care, and consistency will help in showing loyalty. To do this effectively, consistently post content –regardless of if you need to publish at particular weekdays or you upload a few posts each day. Pick one and stick to it, so your followers will know when your posts will come in.

If you need to go on a break, that is not a problem, but ensure you let your followers know about it. For instance, if you are going on a trip, inform them beforehand and tell them you can't wait to be back. You can also let them be aware that you may not keep to schedule during your absence. Doing this proves that you respect the connection with them and their time.

Similarly, to show care and concern, prove to them that their opinions are significant. If they leave comments, do not ignore them. Prove that you care about them each day, similarly as you do about your friends around you.

Invite them to A Personalized and Entertaining Event

You should learn to treat your followers like royalty. People are most likely to purchase from brands that give them the best treatment. For example, you can invite your Instagram followers to a live session where you will provide responses to their questions in your area of experience.

Let them know that you will be responding to questions from the first 20 or 30 people as the case may be. Don't forget to inform them of the time you will be available to respond to their questions.

You can also request that followers send their questions to your DM in advance if they are unable to meet the allocated date/time. In addition to being beneficial to them, it also ensures that you can begin the event seamlessly because you don't need to hold on for someone to ask a question. Instead, the first 10 minutes can be devoted to answering questions from the DM.

Develop Exclusive Deals for your Followers

Let your followers know they are unique. By creating exclusive deals, your followers will keep coming back repeatedly. You don't need to create excessively complex deals, let them be fun and straightforward as it tends to work better.

For instance: "If you purchase a (specific) item today, you will get a 30% off – Exclusive to our Instagram followers. Send us a mail and let us know you saw this post!

Also, you can begin a deal of the week. All of these will ensure followers continue to come back and check in to see what is new. And whenever they do need a service or product you sell, you will be the first they come running to.

Promote Your Followers

Doing this is a fantastic way to gain credibility, give back, and strengthen relationships. The instant you have developed a good relationship; followers transform into customers.

Choose a specific weekday on your Instagram page to advertise a follower. You can use a hashtag of your choice like #followerappreciation and promote a follower. To effectively do this, don't include numerous followers in a single post, as this makes it random and not personal.

Instead, pick a follower that you engage with a lot and make a post about him/her letting them know why their connection is significant to you. To go further with this, you can leave the first comment explaining why you appreciate them and the value they have added to you.

Run Contests on Instagram

Contests are a great way to get leads from Instagram. Not only do people love competing against one another, but they also love free prizes.

First, you need to come up with a great theme. Most contests are successful because they correspond with something the followers have in mind already. So let your contest be centered around a specific season or holiday. Ensure you communicate the prize to be won and that it is substantial enough to urge your followers to partake in the contest. A great technique is to pick a prize that your target market will find appealing.

To take things further, you can add an element of voting. This could be in the lines of: "Whoever gets 500 likes wins a prize". Including this is beneficial to you because it ensures you have a higher chance of trending because of your content, which in turn provides an increase in your brand awareness. The reason is simple; people participating in the contest will inform their family and friends to turn in votes, and the friends will also inform their friends and so on. This can be a great way to get leads as someone who is in search of a service you render may just be directed to your page.

Leverage Testimonials

You are more likely to get a customer from your followers if one or more of your followers have something great to say about their experience with your business.

Take note of the good things people say about your business and request their permission to share on your page. When you share testimonials, it reminds your followers that you offer a specific product or service. Also, it lets others know that those that did business with you found your products or services to be of value.

Take Advantage of Shoppable Posts

It can be quite frustrating to hold onto a customer and get them to take the step of heading to your website and making a purchase decision. However, with the new shoppable post feature, you can now redirect your followers to your product page directly from a post. Simply put; your posts will be like a standard post, but you will have the capacity to tag products on it.

It is less complicated for your prospective clients and followers to see the product, as opposed to heading to your site on their own and searching manually for an item. With a shoppable post, you can turn your followers into customers as the posts will come with the price and link to buy a product. What is left for a customer will be to hit the tag, and they will be diverted to the page of the product.

Strike a Balance

Not many people will buy from you if all you do is continuously promote new products or redirect your followers to your website. Many people won't even stick around in the first place. The same applies to any strategy you choose. Doing the same thing continuously can become predictable and even boring after a while.

But if you continue to switch things and create a balance between promotion, and interaction, then your followers will be happy to continue the interaction later. They will always look forward to what you have to share each day.

Chapter 11

Taking Advantage of Stories and

Contests on Instagram

Instagram stories like we have covered earlier, shares a lot of similarities with Snapchat. With this feature, you can share videos and images which will vanish 24hours after being uploaded. However, Instagram stories can provide an avenue for brands and marketers to get to a more significant number of people, if done the right way.

According to Instagram, stories have urged users to spend more time on the platform and pay more frequent visits. Users less than the age of 25 spend over 32 minutes daily on Instagram, while the older age groups spend over 24 minutes daily on the platform ("22+ Instagram Statistics That Matter to Marketers in 2019", 2019).

This feature offers you a few seconds to prove to millions of individuals that your service or product is worth it, so how do you do it in a way that will ensure conversions? The tips below can help you begin.

Integrate Polls in Instagram Stories

Individuals and brands now can include engaging polls to their stories. In addition to being entertaining, these polls are a great means of engaging with your audience and getting their opinions on various subjects. By taking advantage of the change to get the opinion of your audience on a decision or subject, you could help save money, energy, and time which could be channeled to other areas of your business.

On Travel Tuesday, Airbnb requested that its audience took part in a poll. As straightforward as it seemed, it was well-organized and very professional. Airbnb leveraged the content followers generated, thereby achieving two objectives simultaneously: Airbnb interacts with the content of its followers, and the job of developing a Story becomes less demanding by taking the content already in existence ("Top 10 Successful Hashtag Campaigns That Created an Impact", 2019).

Many brands and influencers have experienced a rise in stories engagement and Instagram live since they started taking advantage of the polls feature. With the help of Instagram insights, they can monitor engagement for entire feeds or per post during a specific period.

Take Advantage of Links

One of the fantastic perks of social media is the intimate relationship brands will create with their followers. Stories have given your brand the chance to take this intimacy a bit further. But, if your brand is not taking advantage of the attention stories provide, then this connection goes down the drain. The least difficult method of leveraging this attention is via direct links.

A significant aspect of Instagram Stories for business is the capacity to link and tag. Using this great feature, you are privy to link your pages. If you are a marketer, you can link product pages where your audience can make purchases immediately. When viewers of your stories swipe up, they get redirected to the page of your choice. As a marketer, you can also link forms for lead generations from any of your marketing software, to add more numbers to your email list. This feature can only be accessed by business profiles that have over 10,000 followers. If you don't meet this criterion, you can choose the option of including a short URL or place a link in your bio which may not be as effective. However, the possibilities at your disposal here are quite enormous.

Tell an Actual Story of Your Brand

The introduction of stories has proven that there is significant value in authentic content in the eyes of your audience. For this reason, when you document your journey, your brand becomes more approachable.

This means you need to use your stories to tell a real story. Tell stories concerning the services and products you provide. This can help in developing the loyalty of brands, which increases the possibility of referrals and purchase.

Perfect instances of digital storytelling include factories showing how a specific product is developed, restaurant showing how specific meals are prepared and makeup brands showing how to tutorials. You have the power to be as creative as you can while doing this.

Use Overlay Text to Magnify CTAs

Typically, you can find the CTA beneath the screen. However, it is quite little and not difficult to miss. Ensure your viewers are aware of what action you need them to take by leveraging on text overlay to recap the CTA in large and bold lettering.

When you develop your stories, ensure you pick the appropriate CTA button that you want to show up. The words you choose, the size of your letters, and the text color can have a lot of impact on if viewers check out your site, sign up or become actual leads. As a marketer, you can include active verbs like "Buy Now." However, if your goal is to generate leads, you can utilize "Sign up Today" etc.

Leverage Instagram Takeovers

Instagram takeovers are fast, fun, and easy methods for boosting your following either by taking control of another user's Instagram account or letting them take control of yours, usually for a period of 24-hours. This is a fantastic way of developing a relationship which is mutually beneficial between your brand and another influencer. Also, it offers an amazing means for growing your audience. The possibilities are limitless.

An easy way for you to do this for your brand or company is to pick a person in your organization to post stories showing how a typical day is for them. Better still, you can collaborate with other brands in the same field as you to trade stories for the day. This will aid in diversifying your content and ensure your clients keep heading back for more.

By aligning your brand with someone who has something of value to add to your desired objective, it encourages genuinely and helps you connect with followers who want to interact with your brand, which in turn makes your network broader.

Utilize Instagram Story Ads

In January 2017, Instagram kick-started the Stories ad function with brands like Airbnb, Netflix, and Nike. Later in March, this feature was opened to various sizes of organizations. When developing your ad, it is vital to quickly get the attention of your followers or audience. Photo ads only remain for 10 seconds, while video ads have a 15 seconds time frame before they vanish.

What this means is that you need to make certain that you can pass across the message effectively during the first seconds of your ad, to enable them to take a step the moment it is done. You need to keep the user interested with powerful visuals, keep them engaged with flawless messaging, and subtly nudge them into taking action.

If you decide to go with photo ads, make sure you utilize a photo which is bright and bold. It should also have simple messaging and clear branding. The user needs to be able to tell with ease who you are, what you do, and how you can assist them fast before the end of the ad. If you meet all of the conditions, your Instagram Stories can quickly go viral, and you don't want to ensure you don't exhaust your budget. To curb this, you need to be on the lookout to ensure you don't go past your daily limit.

Why You Need to Begin Using Instagram Stories Ads

Instagram Stories ads are ideal for reaching new audiences and advertising your business, brand, and products to an audience which is already engaged. Instagram Stories already has a very high rate of Engagement, with Instagram stating that one out of five stories gets a DM from viewers.

Instagram Stories ads are a vital aspect of any Instagram marketing strategy, and it gives you the chance to be as creative as you can. If you are using stories and getting a great level of engagement from them, then there is nothing stopping you from taking advantage of Instagram Stories ads as well. Instagram stories ads offer you a range of options to choose from which include:

- Video ads: These play for 15 seconds before they vanish. You can edit one of your own, or create on via the Ads manager or Facebook's Creative Hub.

- Photo: A motionless image ad which will last for 5 seconds. You can upload one of your designs, or create on via the Ads manager or Facebook's Creative Hub.

- Carousel: These allow you to play as much as three content pieces in a single ad. This could be photos and videos in one ad.

Now that you know what Instagram Stories ads, let's look into some few things to add in your design, and how you can kick-off your first ad campaign on Instagram Stories.

Create a Plan for Your Ad Design

You need to understand that users have the choice of skipping Instagram Stories ads, so this implies that the video and image you integrate into the ad is appealing enough to instantly draw the attention of your viewers.

In designing your ad, you can get the help of an experienced designer or advertising agency that knows how the platform works. You can also develop the ad by yourself with the help of visual design tools.

If you make the choice of using a single image to design your ad, you need to ensure you begin with a high-quality visual. Next, include straightforward but commanding text on the image. An image ad vanishes in 10 seconds, so you need to ensure the message you want to pass is clear. Let your viewers understand what your business does and how you can offer them this service.

It is recommended by Facebook that the size of your image is 1080 x 1920, with a 9:16 aspect ratio. If you would rather go with the option of videos as opposed to an image, ensure your video is in MP4, MOV or GIF format, with a length of no more than 15 seconds. The video can have a size as large as 2.3 GB with no lower than 720p resolution. Note that you will be able to use text like messages, descriptions, title, and other captions.

The instant you have a final video or image you plan on utilizing in your ad, you can now head to the process of developing your Instagram Stories campaign.

Develop Your Ad

In the development of your Instagram Stories ad, you can take advantage of either Power Editor or the Facebook Ads Manager. When you develop your ad, what you need to do first is to pick a campaign objective. Presently, the only objective you can pick for this sort of campaign is Reach. But according to Facebook, later on, there will be other objectives available like Mobile App Installs, Website Clicks, and Web Conversions, among others.

Next, provide your campaign with a name and hit Continue. The instant you are through defining your campaign audience, head to placements, and choose the option for Edit Placements. Then, pick stories under Instagram. Remember that after choosing Stories, the other placements will no longer be checked because you won't be able to run an Instagram Stories ad for any other placement.

After setting up your scheduling or budget, you can then move on to designing your ad. First, you have to select the format for your ad. You can choose to utilize a single video or single image for your ad. Once your selection has been made, the next step is to upload your video or image file. If you choose to go with a video upload, you will be provided with an option to select a preview image when you are finished with the upload.

After you are through with your media upload, you can find out if you want to enter tags or track your campaign. Then, you can now kick-off your campaign. Now, let's move on to how you can leverage contests for your brand.

How Can Brands Take Advantage of Contests?

Determining how you can kick-off a positive contest on Instagram is not as straightforward as other strategies on the platform. The great thing about contests is that they take advantage of UGC (User-generated content) and do not need as much devotion from individuals involved in it.

Lots of users are eager to jump on an offer to win a free flight to their dream destination for posting a selfie with a hashtag or uploading a specific picture. This is what makes Instagram contests appealing and one of the most effective strategies to enhance engagement and boost your audience fast. From lots of appealing freebies to free trips, there are lots of directions your Instagram contest can take.

The Benefit of Instagram Contests for Brands

Instagram is already perfectly set-up for UGC campaigns. Users are already distributing their videos and photos on Instagram. If you can look for a means by which your brand can deviate those existing habits and interest **to where you want them**, you will have the means of engaging users on Instagram in a relevant and entertaining way.

Integrating Instagram contents in your strategy for marketing can aid you in boosting your follower count, broadening your reach, and developing loyal ambassadors for your brand. In this section, we will be looking into a few things that can make your Instagram contest a success.

Plan Your Goals and Objectives

It is vital for you to make a comprehensive plan before you go to a marketing contest on Instagram. For a contest to be a success, its goal must be one that is in line with the behaviors and interests of your target audience.

Regardless of what your objectives are, it is vital that you put a precise goal in place, so you are aware of the contest was a success or not. To aid in streamlining your focus, consider the audience you want to reach. Ask yourself the following:

- What types of posts do they love to see on your account?

- What types of posts do they like to post on their feeds?

- How is their behavior on the platform?

If your goal is to increase your engagement, you should focus on building your purpose and content around content that your followers already want to interact with or post.

Remember to put a budget and time-frame in place for your contest, because deciding these details in advance will aid you in designing a more effective contest.

Put an Entry Method in Place

There are numerous ways for you to develop contests on Instagram, even though the most engaging and efficient contests on Instagram are those that urge your followers to upload photos of their own. Due to this, it is vital for you to create your guidelines and let your audience know what they require to be a part of the contest.

Below are a few concepts you can use as entry methods for your contests:

- Get your followers to upload a video or image to Instagram using a particular theme or hashtag.

- Get your audience to follow you alongside uploading a post, or get them to follow you alone.

- Get your followers to tag your brand in a post they upload.

- Get your audience to comment or like one of your posts.

Ensure you properly plan what the rules are for partaking in the contest, and try to be certain that they are explicitly stated during your promotion. Perhaps the contest has to do with a hashtag not consisting of your brand name. If you want to get recognition for your brand by getting followers to tag your brand, it needs to be explicitly stated in your guidelines.

Locate the Ideal Hashtag

A great hashtag is a foundation for any engaging Instagram contest. In the absence of this, there will be no connection between the generated content and the contest itself. What this implies is that hashtags can help in developing contest or brand recognition by acting as a tool for driving participation or sharing.

However, the problem is that it can be difficult to develop the appropriate hashtag. If you are going to include a timeframe for your contest, you need to develop a hashtag that you won't want to utilize recurrently. Also, many people create hashtags every day, and this might make it a tedious task to get an appealing and unique hashtag.

To aid you in creating the ideal fit for your contest hashtags, the following are a few guidelines to consider:

- Brief: Develop a hashtag that remains in the mind of followers. The easier it is to read and identify your hashtag, the more ideal it is for your contest.

- Significant: Ensure any hashtags you are creating relates to the product, services, or name of your brand. If you decide to go with something general, already with a lot of crowd, it may be challenging to determine the individuals taking part in your contest.

- Unforgettable: There is a huge possibility that users will come across adverts for your contest beforehand. What this implies is that your hashtag has to be easy and catchy enough for users to remember it later on. Put efforts into ensuring your hashtag is easy to write, not difficult to search and appealing enough. Stay away from difficult spellings and a strange choice of words.

- Global: Put your audience in mind. Do all of them use the same kind of words or speak one language? If your audience is global, ensure you exercise caution in using terms specific to a particular region which may confuse others from other areas.

- Uncommon: Investigate before picking a hashtag. Are a lot of individuals utilizing your selected hashtag for other uses? If this is the case, you may want to find something else.

Put a Theme in Place

Lots of contents on Instagram are based on UGC. For this reason, it is vital for you to choose a theme, so your audience understands the kind of videos and pictures they have to post.

Preferably, you will want to go with a theme that goes with your product, services, or market. However, you can leverage on seasons, holidays, and events that go with your brand or product.

Determine How You Will Select the Winners

A major aspect of a properly-structured contest is letting your participants know the way you will choose your winners. Many contests winners are chosen using one of the following ways: A jury or by votes: Let's check out how both choices work:

- **By Votes**: A great method of making your contest go vital is to get participants to contend for the most number of likes. If the incentive is great enough, individuals partaking in the contest will be keen on sharing their posts with their friends and loved ones across numerous channels so they can get the highest amount of likes. This approach aids in boosting your reach of audiences. However, this can also affect your contest negatively. This is because you may face the possibility of individuals using "Like bots" to get themselves fake likes. To ensure there are no issues here, you need to place specific guidelines that prevent participants from doing this.

- **Jury**: This method is a much better option than using votes. Using this method, you select a set of professionals to determine the winner as opposed to depending on a voting system. Regardless of the option, you decide to go with, ensure you explicitly state the method you plan to use so participants would know in advance. Lots of brands combine both options to decide the winner.

Pick the Right Reward

When you want to determine the reward for the contest, you need to reflect on your budget, target audience, and the kind of goals you have in place. Don't forget that by requesting your audience takes part in the contest, you are requesting they make a particular action. Similar to other efforts like this, the incentive they stand to gain has to be more than the energy and cost they need to partake in the contest. While not too many people may be awed by the chance to win a free pair of shoes, many of them would be eager to go out of their way for something like an exotic holiday.

The prize should correlate to the action for entry, but should also be in line with what your target interest is interested in. To determine this, ask yourself this question: What would my target audience be keen on having? You may come up with a huge list of responses to this if you don't consider the budget. Yes, many people will be eager for a free trip, but this should not be the focus. The objective is to determine a prize that is relevant and significant to your brand. Many brands take advantage of giveaways, free services, free products, among others. But, it does not hurt to be creative when making a choice.

Develop Terms and Conditions

Remember that when developing a competition with an incentive attached, you must go along with a few legal guidelines. The laws applicable to you may be dependent on your location or the individuals you give the chance to partake in your contest. This means you need to reach out to your legal practitioner for assistance in putting your terms and conditions in place. It is vital for you to create a terms and conditions page.

A few terms commonly added include:

- Rules guiding how to enter

- Rules guiding how a winner is selected

- Contact details and the name of the promoting brand

- Contest dates

- The rules guiding individuals that can partake in the contest

- The date the contest will end, and the winners would be announced

- The time frame for winners to give feedback and get their prizes

- Information about how the prizes will be sent to the winner or claimed

However, you need to go through the promotion guidelines put in place by Instagram to ensure you are in line with their rules.

Do Lots of Promotion

Now that everything is ready, you need to engage in serious promotion for your contest. So what are the ideal platforms to begin your promotion? The good news is that there are a lot of avenues to use. However, below are a few of them to pick ideas from:

- Your website: Write a blog post on your website, including the contest details, and use it as a point for redirecting users to the landing page of your contest.

- Social media platforms: There is no better place to promote events than social media. Take advantage of all your platforms to ensure your garner as many participants as you can to your contest on Instagram.

Chapter 12

How to Get the Help of Influencers

on Instagram

Investing in digital ads can cost a lot of money. This is the reason why promoted posts and endorsements by influencers on Instagram has become more recognized. Besides, as stated by statistics, influencer marketing has one of the most ROIs in comparison to other online promotion techniques.

For this reason, if you want a fast method of getting your brand out there, you need to get the services of a micro influencer. But before we move any further, let's check out what influencer marketing is all about.

Influencer Marketing – What is it?

Influencer marketing is a technique for marketing that has to do with the partnership between brands and popular pages or personalities. Akin to ambassador programs and celebrity endorsements, Instagram marketing capitalizes on the loyal following and massive audience of an influencer. They are typically paid to make posts on Instagram. However, there are situations where the influencers will partner with brands, in return for a few of their products.

Well-established influencers can cost a lot and typically have a following which could get into millions. This may not be budget friendly for brands on Instagram that have just begun. In this case, the option is to go with a Micro-influencer, who does not have as many followers but gets high rates of engagements from their followers.

Why Instagram Influencers?

Marketing on Instagram is quite effective, and this is not shocking. Now, the traditional means of marketing has become quite invasive, while the new strategy of contacting customers via influencers has been verified to be more efficient. Influencers have a high amount of social power among their followers who see them as reliable and trustworthy.

In contrast to the conventional digital ads, which is a one-way form of advertising, promotions, and endorsements by influencers offer an open channel of communication with their followers. It is almost similar to word of mouth (WOM) marketing, which remains a very effective method of marketing today. Related to this, influencer marketing can get across to customers in a more welcoming and approachable manner.

How Does It Work?

Marketing on Instagram with the help of influencers is not as difficult as you may believe. It does not include any platform for campaign management; neither does it consist of any complex ad bidding or buying systems.

To start influencer marketing, all you have to do is:

- Locate an influencer who has followers that aligns with the target audience of your brand.

- Leave a message when you find the influencer of your choice

- Agree as regards payments or gift in kind as compensation for his/her endorsement of your product or brand.

When making a deal with your chosen influencer, ensure you have a time limit in place and utilize a distinct hashtag and code which the influencer will include in their post caption. It is an easy strategy to make sure that you can monitor the influencer marketing campaigns and determine how effective numerous influencers are. Now that you know how it works, how do you find the right influencer for your brand?

Finding the Best Influencers for Your Brand

To find the right influencer, the following are a few tips that can help:

Determine What You Require

Before you even contact any Instagram influencers, you need to have clear goals in place for what you want to achieve with your campaign.

Is your aim to:

- Promote a particular sales event or product?

- Do you want to grow your followers?

- Are you trying to generate brand awareness?

Providing answers to these questions is vital for putting a budget in place and directing your search for the ideal influencers. Note that if you choose to collaborate with a micro-influencer, you won't be privy to the same level of control a traditional ad campaign offers you. This means you will have to let the influencer develop content that aligns with their distinct style and viewers' preferences.

In the end, being keen to provide a bit of creative freedom will make it less difficult to locate influencers and develop a profitable campaign. Now, with these in mind, you can now begin the search for your ideal influencer.

Search Using Hashtags

It is crucial to find an influencer who is relevant to the niche of your brand. Luckily, the search function Instagram offers makes this very easy to search for your ideal influencer. To get the best result, run your search using hashtags.

Use numerous hashtags that are related to the niche of your brand or organization to assemble a list of prospective influencers. When evaluating the results, pick images that you find appealing. Normally, Instagram shows posts that have the most engagement first, and this is a great way to locate high-quality influencers.

Check out every profile on your list to see how properly it aligns with the goals you have set in place for your brand. Take note of the rate of engagement, their frequency of posts, and if they usually post content that aligns with your niche.

Look for Bloggers

Bloggers can offer your brand a broad range of marketing opportunities. This is because well-established bloggers, in addition to making guest posts and running affiliate marketing, usually have a huge following. To find them, all you need to do is run a quick search on Google, specific to a particular industry to aid you in finding the best influencer for you.

As soon as you have located the best list of bloggers you can find, all you need to do is find their Instagram handles on their website or determine if they will make suitable micro influencers for you. If they do, then the next step will be to reach out.

Even if a specific blogger you would have loved to collaborate with does not have the following you are after on Instagram, it is never a waste to locate them. There is a huge possibility that if you make a connection with them, you can still use them to develop content and build trust in your audience.

Look for Those Who Are Open to Collaborations

Because a micro-influencer has a huge following, it does not mean he is available for collaborations or sponsorships. Luckily, lots of influencers offer vital signals in their profile to help you point out if you can collaborate with them.

Now, lots of micro-influencers will put up their contact details on their profile, to make it easier for prospective ad collaborators to reach them. Taking it a bit further by reading the signs will prevent you from wasting valuable time contacting those who don't want to collaborate.

Look in Your Followers

You may not know it, but your present followers on Instagram could be a very valuable resource for finding the right micro-influencer. This is the case so long as you are ready to put in the work and observe.

The people who follow your brand do so because they love what you do, and for this reason, you may not have to put in extra effort to persuade them that it is worth promoting your service or product. They like your brand already!

A lot of your followers will be keen on promoting your brand if you offer them a free sample product or other incentives. However, you need to do your screening the same way you would do normal influencers; they should have no less than 1,000 followers, posts that relate to your niche, and an interactive audience. If you know how to find the right influencers, but still have no idea of how to approach them the right way, you may never get any influencer to collaborate with you.

Approaching Instagram Influencers the Right Way

As we covered earlier, you need to investigate your chosen influencer before you collaborate with them. Taking it a little further, it is a great idea to follow them on Instagram and their other platforms. This will let you know the way they engage with their audience. If you are satisfied with what you see, the next thing is for you to directly engage them.

Your pitch and ideas for your campaign should be in place. Then you can contact them via their page on Instagram. Most times, you will find a link to a website where you can reach out to them. If this is not the case, lots of serious influencers place their contact info on their bio.

Running an Influencer Marketing Campaign

Now, Influencer marketing is now very recognized. Its popularity got so high that Instagram released a new feature known as Brand Partnerships, which caters to brands and influencers.

If you decide to or not to use this new feature, the impact on your campaign may not be so high. However, if you do use it, remember that there are a few partnership policies you need to go with. You can find them here. Ultimately, the vital thing is the technique you use in managing and approaching your strategies in Instagram influencer marketing. To aid you in starting, below are a few steps that you should follow:

Determine Your Audience

The very first thing to have in place even before contacting an Influencer is to have a detailed idea of your target audience. Ensure that the followers of your prospective Instagram influencer closely aligns with your audience.

Another way to do this is to split your audience into numerous groups. For instance, if your brand offers innumerable products to women you can search for influencers in precise niches in the lifestyle space of women like fashion, hair care, makeup, accessories, etc. All of the influencers can then assist in the promotion of various products offered by your brand.

When you categorize your audience, you can reach out to micro-influencers and possibly enhance your rate of engagement and ROI. Also, it will give you the chance to focus on a relevant audience centered around particular products.

Locate the Appropriate Influencer

To find your influencer, use the options we covered above. You can take it further by employing the services of tools like the Keyword tool. To use this, head to the PEOPLE function and input a topic or keyword pertaining to your brand. Then copy out the Instagram influencers from the result. As a recap, searching with hashtags, checking out blogs, and looking into your followers are also great ways to find influencers.

Next, go through each of them and choose only those that are relevant to your brand. If you find suitable choices, check out their pages to see if they suit your needs and make a choice. Picking those with a reasonable amount of following, with high rates of engagement and the same niche as you, will have a lot of impact on your campaign.

Reach Out to the Influencer

As we covered earlier, reach out to the influencer via his/her DM or contact information. They are also humans looking to make some money, so ensure you are polite and professional in your approach.

Measure Your Results

A great campaign for Influencer marketing is incomplete if you don't measure and track results. Regardless of the kind of influencer you decide to go with, or what your payment agreement with them is, you need to be aware of their performance.

By doing an analysis of their numbers like click-through and engagements, you will get a better understanding of which influencer provided better results for your campaign. With the information you get, you will be able to alter your campaign to make sure things go more seamlessly.

Below are a few tips for measuring and tracking your Influencer marketing campaigns on Instagram:

- Utilize a hashtag or unique code to keep track. The influencer includes this in his/her post caption.

- Use bit.ly to shorten links. This will give you the capacity to monitor click performance. This only works for arrangements that need the influencer to place your links in their bio.

- Make a spreadsheet for tracking. You can do this on Google

Sheets or Excel. Then, you add various metrics like Clicks, Impression, Follower Count, and Engagement. With this document, you will have the capacity to monitor your campaign more comprehensively, particularly if you are working with lots of influencers.

Create a different landing page for your promotion on Instagram. After creating the page, install a Google Analytics tracking code. This can be a very effective option if you are running a special campaign.

Influencer marketing is something you can use on numerous social media platforms. You can use it to sell a product, promote a brand, or build your page on Instagram. It is certainly something you should take advantage of if you want your brand to grow higher than it is presently.

Chapter 13

How Does the Instagram Algorithm Work?

The algorithm is a deciding factor of who views your published content and who doesn't. This applies to both SEO and social media. However, these algorithms tend to change frequently, which makes a strategy that was effective before becoming obsolete. For this reason, you need to continuously advance as well.

When it comes to Instagram, especially, posting frequently using the appropriate hashtags won't imply that your content will get to the relevant audience. Rather, you will have to reflect on how to work around the algorithm to diversify your approach to marketing on Instagram. In essence, the value of the algorithm is something you can't underrate, which is what makes it something vital to consider. In this chapter, you will learn the way the Instagram algorithm works and how you can work around it to achieve the best results. Now that you understand what the algorithm is, how exactly does the Instagram algorithm function?

How Does the Instagram Algorithm Function?

The new Instagram algorithm determines the arrangement of the posts that will be viewed by users when they scroll through their feed. Using certain signals, it gives priority to posts, pushing those that are relevant to the top and offering them a high level of visibility, while the less relevant content is moved to the lower end of the user's feed.

Instagram published some information in June 2018, showing a few elements that the algorithm capitalizes on when ranking the content on the feed of users. Although it is vital to understand that the recent algorithm could be altered later in the future, there are still some major factors used to rank a post which you need to consider in your Instagram strategy. They include:

- Connection with the user: If a specific user has engaged with a host of your previous content, they have a higher probability of seeing your recent content. This allows for repeat and continuous engagement on your content, which is vital for the development of loyal followers.

- Level of interest shown by the user: This signal is dependent on if the user engages with other accounts and posts similar to yours when they go through Instagram. In essence, any user who shows interest in content related to yours, has a higher tendency to see posts you make.

- How recent the post was: Previously, Instagram utilized a sequential feed. However, this is no longer the case, but that does not mean the timing is not a factor to date. Posts which were recently uploaded will be pushed above the feed, while less recent posts will come up further below.

Instagram also shared some additional considerations which are vital; they include:

- If users follow numerous accounts, your struggle to get to the top of their feed will be more

- If you are not on the top of the feeds of users who don't stay so long on Instagram or check out the application, the chances of your content been seen are lower.

- In comparison to Instagram business accounts, personal accounts are not instantly at a disadvantage when it has to do with organic reach.

Now that you understand how the Instagram algorithm works, you need to learn how you can alter your strategy to get to more of your clients. To do this, the steps below may be of help:

Don't Focus On Reach Alone, Relationships Matter Too

Loyalty from your audience alongside continuous interaction from those who follow you, now has a higher level of importance, since it will be able to provide you with a spot at the top of their feeds.

There are ways to establish these relationships using your content, some of which include:

- Reminders that urge users to share their opinions and things they feel and offer you a chance to begin a discussion with them.

- Uploading posts that help build engagement, like Instagram contests or tag-a-friend post that urge users to leave comments.

- User-generated content concerning your brands that have been posted by your followers. In addition to aspiring more UGC, users might tag you in the posts they make and further develop your Instagram presence.

However, if you want to make headway on Instagram, you need to think beyond your posts.

Leave Comments On Posts from Brands and Users Relevant to You

You can also interact with the people on their posts to develop relationships beyond your posts, by making relevant and engaging comments on content from influencers pertinent to you, prospective clients, and related organizations.

Also, leaving posts on more established accounts that have a huge following can provide more visibility to your profile and comment as well. Take a look at accounts that the audience you are targeting has a probability to follow, follow these accounts, and become a part of the conversation. If you decide to go through this route, be authentic, and ensure you make relevant comments. Don't just leave non-specific responses or sales pitches. Show the personality of your brand and engage in a relevant manner.

You can take it a step further by turning on post notifications for certain accounts. This will ensure you can leave comments promptly, enhancing the possibility that it will get visibility, thanks to the focus of Instagram feeds on recent posts. To achieve this, it is essential that you are a follower of the account. Tap the three dots at the right-hand angle of the application and hit "Turn on post notifications" to begin getting push notifications the instant they upload a new post.

Upload Posts During Peak Periods

Since the recency of posts is still a major consideration for where your posts will be placed in the feeds of your followers, you need to exploit it. It, not a bad idea to get a huge level of engagement when your post first goes live, and it will inform Instagram that this a post that would love to be seen by a higher number of your followers.

To enhance the possibility of each post you make, make efforts to upload content when your followers are most active. Refer to the steps in Chapter 6 to find the right posting time for you.

Leave Responses to Comments When They Are New

When you leave responses to as many comments as you can, you will enhance your number of comments while boosting further replies. Additionally, it increases your probabilities of getting more engagement while the potential reach of your post is at its highest.

When you respond to comments, it can lead to additional comments from the main poster. Even something as simple as a thank-you can go a long way. However, in some circumstances, you can begin conversations which give you substantial engagement that will aid in increasing the reach of your posts and other posts in the future.

Use Community Hashtags to Get to Users Who Are Active

Instagram hashtags can aid in increasing your reach by ensuring you come up in significant searches. However, if you want this approach to be efficient, you have to pick hashtags that your audience uses in searching for content as well as other users.

Community hashtags, in particular, are quite active. Although they may not have as many posts as the other well-known hashtags, they are already being shared and explored by numerous groups on Instagram who are in search of ways to create connections with others that have an interest in that movement, topic or community.

From here, you will obtain views that can provide you with clicks via your engagement, profile, and prospective followers. Although these relevant hashtags will differ according to industry, it is easy to find them because they define your perfect customer and are constantly filled with new posts related to your niche.

Repost Already Existing Content to Add a New Feel

If you have issues generating adequate content on Instagram to get more pull in terms of traffic, or you want to ensure that particular content gets seen by as many users as possible, a great way to go is to repurpose previous content, especially as your follower base increases.

This will push you leading content to the top feed once more. In addition, those who missed it when you initially posted it will get to enjoy it this time. Although many brands just delete an old post and post it how they previously shared it, repurposing content works differently.

If you have no idea of how to properly repurpose content, the methods below can help:

- Include a caption different from the one you used previously

- Make a video of the past post images

- Integrate new designs into the picture. You can easily do this if you edit the image of the previous post using the various filters available to you on Instagram.

- Use popular hashtags to share your existing content once more like #throwbacktfriday

It can save you a lot of time if you repurpose content. However, you should not rely on it. Remember to diversify, and go through your feed to get rid of duplicate content. Users will still have the capacity to check your previous posts, and you want to make sure they don't come across the same image numerous times.

Utilize Stories to Gain Attention

A lot of marketers focus on Instagram stories because the algorithm they use is not the same as the ones used in the posts on your feed. It is also an amazing method of interacting with your followers and enhancing loyalty. This leads to an increase in engagement on your stagnant posts, which in turn leads to additional reach.

The following are ways to do this:

- Incorporate hashtag stickers to your branded hashtag

- Encourage engagement using interactive stickers

- Share Stories uploaded by other users

- Urge you, users, to put on post notifications

When you do this in the right manner, like subtly sending a reminder to users, it can prove to the algorithm how significant your brand is to your community. Those who turn their notifications on, in addition to seeing more of your content, will have more likelihood of engaging with your posts.

Make Sure Your Posts Are Amazing

Instagram has made it known numerous times that producing amazing content is the only method of increasing the feed ranking of your content. However, Instagram's major appeal has always been the unstated rule that you need high-quality pictures.

So if you want better engagement, this might mean you need to take a different approach. You can get the services of an experienced photographer and find out what you can learn. You can also download new tools that can increase your knowledge of editing photos.

Remember to Develop Relationships

If you want the best Instagram has to offer, you need to do more than regularly post content. Rather, it is vital that you also pay attention to developing a relationship while keeping communication with users on your pot and beyond them.

Social media algorithms tend to change. However, if you take the innovative and change with them, you will learn that there are numerous methods of getting the audience you desire.

Chapter 14

Tracking your ad success on

Instagram

After you have set up your ad campaign and published it, you can relax and hold on for the outcome of your ad. However, it does not stop there. To ensure your Instagram ad is a success, you have to monitor and measure the results and determine if it is a success. Ensuring your ads remain a success after you have put them up, is also as vital as publishing them in the first instance.

In this chapter, you will learn how you can do this using the Facebook Ads manager and some of the most important metrics you need to track.

Instagram Ads Reporting – How to Get Started

Shopify states that posts on Instagram have a 1.08% rate of conversion, which in comparison to other social media platforms like Pinterest with (0.54%), and Twitter with (0.77%), is on the extremely high side ("Instagram Ads Reporting and Optimization – Guide to 10x Results", 2017).

If you are a marketer or a brand trying to break into Instagram, this is certainly great news for you. However, you need to learn how to view the precise ad results of your campaigns on Instagram. The least difficult means of accessing your Instagram ad reports is to sign in the Facebook Ads Manager. Here, all of your campaigns currently running and those that have been completed in the reporting page will be visible.

Remember that you require an Instagram business account to view comprehensive campaign reports. When you navigate to the reports page on the Facebook ad manager, you will be able to categorize your ads by objectives, dates, and so on. You can also zoom in to a particular campaign to measure how all the ads you put up are performing.

To choose a campaign, you need to click on the checkbox which you can find before the campaign's name. Next, you can head to the Ads tab and Ads set to view how every unit is performing in a specific campaign. If you want to see more metrics, find your way to the Columns page, and choose another report setup.

Campaign Breakdown

Coupled with the campaign metrics that will be displayed in your Ads Manager reports, you can further elaborate on your Instagram ad results with the help of the Breakdown menu.

With the breakdown function, you will be able to screen campaigns using:

- Time: days, weeks, or months

- Delivery: Gender, device location, time, age, browsing platform

- Action: video sound, destination, conversion device, video view type, and so on.

You can choose one criterion from all sections — for instance, one from delivery, and another from time, and so on.

With the report breakdown by placement, you can compare the placement of your Instagram ads against other ad placements, which are currently active. In addition, it offers you answers to lots of other vital questions like:

- What target countries perform the best?

- Which regions come with the most Instagram ads cost?

- What device users have the highest rate of conversions?

- What time of the weekend or days offer the highest conversions at the least cost?

To further split your campaigns using various criteria, you need to select one Facebook Campaign or more. Then, pick a criterion from the breakdown menu. If you are going through the Facebook Ads reports for the first time, it can seem very confusing, because there are lots of data you probably don't know how to summarize. The tips we covered above can make it less difficult, but with experience, it gets much easier.

Vital Metrics You Need to Track

To further ensure you are successful, below are some essential metrics you need to keep track of, so you can see how well your ads are performing.

Relevance Score of Instagram Ads

A relevance score is a number between 1-10 which aids you in understanding the reaction some specific ads is getting from your audience. This metric is calculated by Facebook for each of your ads, using the three core factors below:

- Is your ad performing properly? Are you getting the conversions you optimized for?

- Negative feedback from those who come across your ad. For instance, when a person hits, "I don't want to see this," the instant your ad comes up.

- Positive feedback from those who come across your ad. For instance, clicks, views, app installs, and so on.

You can view the relevance score of your Instagram ads in the Facebook Ads Manager reports. All you have to do is pick "Performance and Clicks."

When you have a relevance score between 1-3, it implies that the Instagram ads are not really relevant to the audience you are targeting. But a score of 6 and above can drastically reduce your cost of advertising. This is because Facebook will give them priority over other ads in competition with yours, and would deliver your ads to a much broader audience. To enhance your relevance score, you can update your Instagram copywriting or ad design. Better still, you could employ another form of Instagram ad targeting.

Number of Conversions

The number of ad conversions and impressions is also another important metrics you need to look into. If you notice any ad that seems to be doing very well in regard to the rate of conversion and cost per click, but only delivered a few conversions, then it is not an ad which is doing well. To view the number of Instagram ad conversions, clicks, and impressions, as before you need to pick the "Performance and Clicks" section from the menu.

Conversion Rate

Your conversion rate is another important campaign metric you want to monitor in your Instagram reports. Conversion rate shows how large a fraction of the users who check out the ad and convert on your bargain. You define the conversion in the setup phase of the campaign. This could include signups, link clicks, purchases among a host of others.

To see the average rate of conversion of your ad, you will have to do some simple calculation. Divide the number of conversions by that of ad impressions, then multiply the sum by 100.

(CPC) Cost Per Conversion

Similar to your conversion rates, if your ads are having a great click-through-rate, but don't convert, then you won't attain any new clients. This is why the CPC is your most vital campaign metric. It lets you learn the amount a conversion actually costs you.

To see the CPC metric, you have to define the conversion for your ad campaign during the process of setup.

Instagram Ad Frequency

This displays the amount of time an average user in your audience has viewed your ad. If the frequency of your ad gets beyond 4 points, it implies that members of your audience have viewed your ad numerous times and have probably gotten tired of it.

To find out your ad frequency, navigate to the Facebook Ads Manager, select a campaign, and pick the Delivery view in the reporting page.

From here, you can view a campaign's ad frequency, and set your chosen ad level in the column for reporting.

How Does the Data in Your Instagram Reports Help You?

The ability to get information concerning how your ads are performing at a comprehensive level is of huge benefit. You can utilize your reports in optimizing your ads in numerous ways, which include:

- The kinds of ads that have the best or worst performance

- The period of the day, your audience is at its peak, or when your level of engagement is higher, to enable you to take advantage of the dayparting options Instagram provides.

- The ad creative that has the best or worst performance

- The demographic areas with the best or worst performance

- The countries with the best or worst performance

In essence, every option you are provided with when setting up your ad is something you can experiment with. You are also privy to a look at the metrics that have the best and worst performance. With this information, you can prevent a campaign from falling apart by getting rid of the ad or device with the worst performance, or any measurement your report proves is setting your campaign up to fail.

Chapter 15

Growth Strategies for Brands on

Instagram

Now, Instagram is one of the top recognized social channels on the net. As we have mentioned earlier, it is a good place for individuals to share, create, and connect with their friends and the brands they love. It is known that 80% of Instagram users follow a business on the platform.

Similar to other social channels, a brand with the goal of getting the best Instagram has to offer, requires a decent amount of following. An increase in the number of followers means enhanced credibility, more engagement, and a better presence online.

However, the issue is that growth on Instagram goes beyond a game of numbers. Organizations are leveraging on the $6.48 billion value of profit churned out from Instagram each year by creating genuine connections with individuals who pay a visit to their pages ("US AD Spending", 2019). However, if a brand is aiming to grow, it is vital for the growth to be organic. Let's learn why below.

Why Must the Growths of Brands On Instagram Be Organic?

Many people have tried purchasing brands at some point in time. These include celebrities, influencers, and even politicians.

As a newcomer on Instagram, convincing your customers that you are valuable to them when you have only a few followers can be very difficult. But, if you have a huge amount of followers, your credibility seems to spike. However, going with the crowd and doing what others are doing won't get you anywhere. When you pay for followers, it means numbers are the only thing that will be added to your account. In essence, the individuals you are posting content for, won't take any practical action on your page. They won't share your content, like your pictures, or purchase your product. Also, buying followers breaches the guidelines of the IG community, which implies that your account could be at risk of a purge.

So, if purchasing followers is out of the question, how do you make yourself unique from the other active organizations on Instagram? The solution to this is quite straightforward; you need to learn to increase your number of followers organically. Below, we shall be covering some strategies that can help you grow on Instagram organically.

Growth Strategies for Brands on Instagram

As a brand on Instagram, there are lots of growth strategies you can implement to increase your follower count. Some of these include:

Make Quality Posts Frequently

Instagram, as we covered earlier, had the most levels of interaction in comparison to other social media platforms. Your followers are available to create connections with you. However, you have to provide something for them to engage with first.

Users are always in search of timeliness and stability from the businesses and brands they follow. Additionally, the Instagram algorithm puts your presence on Instagram into consideration when trying to determine where to place you on the Explore Page. But, when you begin to plan a consistent schedule for posting, you have to attain the right timing as we have covered earlier. It won't be of any benefit for your followers consisting of professionals if you make posts during the day when they would be at work.

It will be essential for you to do your research into information like the habits of your audience to ensure your schedule is ideal for you. Also, to recap, if you don't have time to manage your growth on Instagram consistently while running your business, you can take advantage of some of the tools for scheduling we listed earlier. When you prepare posts before-hand, it makes sure you have a continuous influx of content available, even when you are occupied with other activities.

Offer Your Audience What They Desire

Similar to other authentic strategies for getting organic growth, getting organic growth on Instagram requires amazing content. In the end, if your aim is for people to follow, like, and interact with your page, then you will have to upload content that they find appealing.

So, what methods can you use in determining what your followers anticipate from you? Below are a few ways to do so:

- Observe competitors that have target audiences similar to yours: determine the type of content brands in niches similar to you are posting and point out everything that amasses a high level of engagement. For example, do brands in your niche get better outcomes when they make video posts instead of typical images?

- Monitor the trends: monitor the profiles of influencers and customers in the space as you to determine the trends they have been following or hashtags they are utilizing. Doing this will provide you with an understanding that brings the most engagement among your followers.

- Track your performance with the help of a tool: there are a host of tools like Sprout Social, which you can use to follow keywords that are bringing you the highest amount of traffic and engagement among your followers. This way, you will learn why your posts with the top performance are working and implement the results in your other posts.

If you are having issues picking the appropriate content to get organic growth on Instagram, a great way is to find out from your followers the form of contents they would want to see. You can use the poll feature offered by Instagram to get feedback and ideas from your present customers.

Try Out Various Forms of Media

Do not forget that Instagram goes beyond images alone. Although the images you post each day can help you build your reputation and personality on the platform, you can shake things up a little by checking out other options as well.

For instance, more than 60% of the ad impressions gotten on Instagram are from videos (Vrountas, 2018). Trying story ads increases click-through rate, marketing recall, and buying intent simultaneously. As video content keeps on ruling on Instagram, it can be a great choice to make your feed diversified. Also, with the advent of IGTV, there are more avenues for exploiting videos. To do this, try out the following:

- Behind the scene footage which introduces your team members and develops organic relationships

- Question and Answer sessions with influencers to enhance how credible your brand is

- How-to content that showcases your product's or service's

distinct appeal

Interact with your followers

Similar to all other social media platforms, Instagram has to do with engagement. A lot of brands in the search for Instagram growth, make the mistake of ignoring the social aspect of marketing on social media.

When you post the appropriate content, at the right moment in a consistent manner, it will draw in increased attention from your audience. However, it is the way you communicate with the people in your audience that will transform a typical visitor into loyal fans of your brand.

When you respond to a question, comment, or reply to a DM, they will all aid you in the development of more meaningful relationships with the people you follow. It is not essential that you reply to every mention or message; all you need to do is be as active as you can. Your followers recognize that you have a business to run; however, all conversations you have with them will be appreciated.

Enhance Your Hashtag Tactic

Hashtags are not to be undermined when it comes to attaining organic growth on Instagram. They can effectively induce engagements on your post. Also, users can follow IG hashtags, which makes it less difficult to broaden your reach using the appropriate tags.

However, the guidelines for using hashtags have changed, as now, IG places more emphasis on tags that are relevant and provide your followers with distinct value. Now, it is not possible to expect results if you post the same ten tags on each of your photos. Rather, you have to locate the appropriate blend of tags for every post that can enhance your image.

To get the best outcomes, experiment with:

- Branded Hashtags: Utilize the name of your organization or a distinct tag to build your brand's engagement. More than 60% of the hashtags on Instagram are branded (West, 2019).

- Current tags: Take a look at the tags that are coming up on the explore page of Instagram. Do any of them apply to your content or brand? Consider including them to your posts to make your reach broader.

- Location tags: Posts incorporated with geotags get more engagement than others. This is as high as 79 percent. To find geotag, check out the top left part of your post (West, 2019).

- Recognized hashtags: Although #TBT and #Love, are well-known hashtags and may be difficult to get good rankings with, they can still fit in some forms of content. Try including a few well-known tags to your stories and images.

Boost more User-Generated Content (UGC)

If you are having issues attaining measurable growth on Instagram, you can look into your present followers for help. Customers have a higher likelihood of purchasing from a brand their peers suggest to them. Also, tags and mentions from your client can aid you in reaching a new audience that you typically won't have found yourself.

There are numerous methods of developing UGC. An easy option is to begin a competition using a branded hashtag. Offer your clients the opportunity to win a special price if they upload and share a picture of themselves using your product, tag people they know in the comments, or follow your profiles.

The instant you pick a victor for your contest, you can gain access to a higher number of user-generated content by requesting that your customers showcase their prize or post a review on their profile. Do not forget that giveaways require:

- An appealing reward

- A way of keeping track of entries

- Promotional tags and branded hashtags

Grow Some Influence

It can be difficult to learn how to organically boost your followers on Instagram. It takes a lot of time to get genuine progress because you have to get the respect of a customer and show how credible you are in a competitive marketplace. A great method of instantly pushing your efforts ahead is to take advantage of the influence someone in the same niche as you already possesses.

Using Influencer Marketing is a seamless method of amplifying the voice of your brand on Instagram. With the appropriate influencer, you capitalize on the trust already in existence between an Instagram user and his/her followers, to broaden the reach of your brand. Locate influencers in your niche by looking for hashtags in your industry, and start to develop a relationship with them fast.

Do not forget that there is a proper way to reach out to influencers. Don't just go in and request for a shout-out immediately. Rather, leave comments on their contents, mention them on posts you make and send them free samples of your products. Ultimately, you and the influencer should come to an agreement.

Get Attention Beyond Instagram

Lastly, don't forget to push traffic back to your profile on Instagram from other online locations. Don't conclude that the individuals who follow you on Twitter and Facebook are also aware that you have an active Instagram account. Leave links redirecting users back to your posts on Twitter and Facebook, place your branded hashtag in emails and take a screenshot of images on your Instagram profile to be included in your blog posts.

The higher the level of attention you draw back to your Instagram page from other avenues on the web, the more the reach of your brand. Also, when you develop your presence on other platforms, you may enhance your trustworthiness enough to get an opportunity to be verified on Instagram.

A few methods of promoting your IG channel on other platforms include:

- Being a guest writer on blogs significant to your audience

- Including details of your Instagram profile in your email campaigns

- Turning in press releases alongside links to your account on Instagram

- Mention your posting links and hashtags on other platforms of social media.

It is not easy to determine how to build your followers organically. But it does not mean it can't be done. The top accounts on Instagram invest a huge amount of effort and time in creating it. This is the reason many brands choose to take the easy way out, one of which is to purchase followers.

Don't fall into temptation. Remember that even though this may initially feel like a great idea, it would have no positive effect on your business. Rather, ensure you pay attention to careful content development, organic growth, and continuous measurement.

Chapter 16

Spying On Your Competitors

Ethically

Competition is vital in every area of life, and Instagram is not exempted. Even if you believe you have no competition, the truth is that some other individual out there is offering the same service as you. So never underestimate the requirements of individuals as they are the same in all aspects of the globe.

So if you are the only one providing a service in a specific region, remember to look for likely competitors around you or in other countries aside from yours. But how can you determine what your competition is doing on social media, specifically Instagram? How do you learn about their behaviors or strategies? Are these answers even essential to you?

Put simply; the answer is yes. You should have an interest in all of these details and understand each of them so you can use the results you attain to build your page on Instagram. In this chapter, you will be learning how to spy on your competition regardless of where they are situated. But first. Let us look into why you need to spy on your competitors ethically.

Why Do You Need to Spy?

Simply put, you have to learn about your opponent if you want to do better than them. It is also a means of getting inspiration and ideas for how you can promote your brand and grow it. Below are a few ways ethically spying on your competitors can assist you:

- Learn where they excel and where they don't: By spying on your Instagram competitors, you will be able to learn the areas they are excelling in and how you can do better from them. Also, by learning the areas they have no success, you will be able to pick lessons from their errors and ensure you don't do the same things.

- Find out the kind of content they are sharing: By spying, you will learn if your competition has better content than you, or if they are getting more engagement on Instagram than you do. Then, you can learn about the kind of content to provide and which to stay away from for the best engagement. This way, you eradicate the need for wasting time alongside trial and errors when you want to engage with your audience since you have an insight into what works and what does not.

- What method of promotion do they use for their brands? Spying on your competition can show you the marketing strategies they currently employ. You will also learn if it is providing them the results they desire. Since they are in the same niche as you, and you both are after the same target audience, whatever works for them would most likely work for you. Better still, you can improve their strategy and be better than they are.

- Learn what their activity on social media is like: What is their level of engagement? When you spy on your competition, you can learn the amount of engagement and if it is more than yours. Also, you will learn if their number of followers is increasing at a faster rate than yours and the reason behind this. With the results, you can learn what you are doing wrong and step ahead of the competition.

Now that we have covered these, below are a few ways to spy on your Instagram competitors.

Take Advantage of Unique Tools That Monitor Your Competition on Instagram

There are numerous methods of spying on your competition, but you can take advantage of tools to help you with it. Using a tool like Brand24 can help you take the work off your hands while you channel your energy to other areas.

Develop a profile and begin to create a project for your brand. In addition to this, create one for your competitors. It is not difficult to utilize and is an easy and amazing method to spy on their activities, their mentions, and the effect they have on their network. Brand24 lets you pick the profiles you want to follow for your competition and your brand. For instance, utilize Instagram as the network of your choice, and you will be able to view all of the mentions the users convey all through social media that have to do with your competitors and your business.

Take advantage of tools to take the work off your hands so you can pay attention to your technique, so you can ensure it is more enhanced than that of your competitors. Some other examples of some of these tools include:

- Sprout Social

- Phlanx

- Social Blade etc.

Follow Your Competition On Instagram

When you follow your competition on Instagram, you will be able to monitor how they communicate with their audience. Also, you can benefit from the tricks and tips they don't directly offer. However, remember to use another profile to follow them, because they will know you are spying on them if you use your brand profile.

By following your competitors on Instagram, you see what they share and like. You also see how they respond to contents. Even if the competition is in another county, the idea still stays the same, and you can easily tap from them.

It is vital to observe the way your competitors behave naturally with followers they know or don't know. The idea is to see the value they offer their audience.

When you follow your competition on Instagram, you learn the following:

- The kind of posts they employ to reach their clients and audience on Instagram. Various organizations employ a host of descriptions and slogans in their posts. But when looking into your competitors, it is vital for you to learn the keywords they integrate into their posts. Aside from keywords, you can check out the terms and wordings of their posts and how long their captions are. Ideally, for the best engagement, captions should consist of 138-150 characters.

- Frequency of posts and best posting time. Understanding the frequency of posting by your competitors is vital. By following them secretly, you can learn their posting times and see the level of engagements they are getting.

The outcome of your investigation will help you learn when to post your content. You will also find out the kinds of filters they are using and get inspiration to create something better on your page.

Follow their Instagram Stories Using a Fake Account

As we covered above, you want to be subtle about it when following your completion on Instagram. They may know who runs the business profile, so it's best to use a random account and follow their Instagram Stories and posts. This is more essential when it comes to Instagram stories since they will be able to tell who checked out their stories.

However, remember that any form of content, regardless of if it is a story, photo, or video is tailored to a precise audience. This means you can easily adjust it to fit your audience as well. But, you need to remember not to copy and repost it directly. Instead, get inspiration from it. Check out the kind of audience they have, what they engage with, and who they follow; then you develop a similar content for Instagram.

Run a Search for Their Branded Hashtags on IG

In addition to following their accounts, you have to do some investigation of your own. Follow posts made by your competition and take note of the precise set of hashtags they utilize. Look through Instagram for the hashtags to learn who else is utilizing it and create connections with them.

To succeed when marketing on social media, having a branded should go a long way. If you know this, your competitors will certainly know this too and would have branded hashtags. To make your task easier, you need to learn the hashtag they capitalize on the most. When you do, run a search for it on Instagram, learn how they interact with those who follow them, and how the audience responds. You can observe your competitors to learn the appropriate hashtags you can integrate into your content, so it gets to a broader market.

It is also vital to find out the active users or influencers who upload posts on Instagram with the hashtag of your competitors. This will keep you informed on the hashtags to employ on your posts. If you utilize the right mix of hashtags in your posts, you can make it easy to discover your brand, which in turn enhances your engagement on Instagram.

Websta and Pixlee are great tools that can help you with it. Also, you can use the search explorer on Instagram. This is a very seamless way of learning how your competition acts on Instagram and how they are viewed by their audience.

Takeaway

Competition is not a bad thing. It makes you want to get better than you are. If you were the only one providing a service without any competition, you won't strive to become better and will continue to repeat the same thing over and over until your audience gets tired or bored.

However, with the presence of competition, you become aware of how you can better serve your audience. You also get the desire to understand what their wishes are and how you can make it happen.

If you understand how to deal with competition, and use it for your benefit, it will be more of a positive thing for your brand instead of negative. Spy on your competition ethically, observe how they act, respond and communicate with their audience, adapt and do better than they are doing, and with time, you will grow to lengths you never imagined possible.

Conclusion

Instagram has proven to us how valuable visuals can be. It has provided numerous amounts of brands and individuals an amazing platform to market themselves and their brands.

It is only essential that you exploit what Instagram offers you and you are bound to get to where you desire. If you are just signing-up on Instagram for the first time, the truth is, you will have to channel a huge amount of effort to make yourself unique.

In this book, I have covered a lot of information that you can take in and implement to make your Instagram journey an easy one, even if you are a newcomer to the platform. All that is left is for you to remain creative and come up with unique strategies to pull loyal fans and followers.

So why wait? Take the step today.

Bibliographies

22+ Instagram Statistics That Matter to Marketers in 2019. (2019). Retrieved from https://blog.hootsuite.com/instagram-statistics/

33 Mind-Boggling Instagram Stats & Facts for 2018. (2019). Retrieved from https://www.wordstream.com/blog/ws/2017/04/20/instagram-statistics

Balakrishnan, A., & Boorstin, J. (2017). Instagram says it now has 800 million users, up 100 million since April. Retrieved from https://www.cnbc.com/2017/09/25/how-many-users-does-instagram-have-now-800-million.html

Chi, C. (2019). When Is the Best Time to Post on Instagram in 2019? [Cheat Sheet]. Retrieved from https://blog.hubspot.com/marketing/instagram-best-time-post

Clarke, T. (2019). 22+ Instagram Statistics That Matter to Marketers in 2019. Retrieved from https://blog.hootsuite.com/instagram-statistics/

Dunn, B. (2019). Retargeting - How One Campaign Generated Me 16,900% ROI. Retrieved from https://ppcmode.com/traffic/retargeting

Enterprise, F. (2019). Social Media Case Studies & Client Stories | Sprout Social. Retrieved from https://simplymeasured.com/blog/adidas-wins-with-instagram-how-the-brand-doubled-followers-in-under-3-months/#sm.00o09am0pymue7t10aq2nohh77wzk

Friedman, M. (2015). Which Photo Filters Get the Most "Likes" on Social Media?. Retrieved from https://www.harpersbazaar.com/culture/news/a10979/yahoo-georgia-tech-flickr-photo-filters/

Global Instagram user age & gender distribution 2019 | Statistic. (2019). Retrieved from https://www.statista.com/statistics/248769/age-distribution-of-worldwide-instagram-users/

Global Cosmetic Products Market Will Reach USD 863 Billion by 2024: Zion Market Research. (2019). Retrieved from https://globenewswire.com/news-release/2018/06/22/1528369/0/en/Global-Cosmetic-Products-Market-Will-Reach-USD-863-Billion-by-2024-Zion-Market-Research.html

How much is the travel industry worth? Try US$5.29 trillion - Travelweek. (2019). Retrieved from http://www.travelweek.ca/news/how-much-is-the-travel-industry-worth-try-us5-29-trillion/

Instagram Ad Costs: The Complete Updated Resource for 2018. (2018). Retrieved from https://adespresso.com/blog/instagram-ads-cost/

Instagram Ads Reporting and Optimization – Guide to 10x Results. (2017). Retrieved from https://karolakarlson.com/instagram-ads-reporting/

Johnson, T. (2019). The Ultimate Guide To Amazon Baby Products. Retrieved from https://www.cpcstrategy.com/blog/2019/05/amazon-baby-products/

Price, E. (2012). Facebook Buys Instagram for $1 Billion. Retrieved from https://mashable.com/2012/04/09/facebook-instagram-buy/

Pet Care Market Size Worth $202.6 Billion By 2025 | CAGR: 4.9%. (2018). Retrieved from https://www.grandviewresearch.com/press-release/global-pet-care-market

Social Media Case Studies & Client Stories | Sprout Social. (2019).

Retrieved from https://simplymeasured.com/blog/adidas-wins-with-instagram-how-the-brand-doubled-followers-in-under-3-months/#sm.000o9am0pymue7t10aq2nohh77wzk

Schmidt, S. (2018). 4 Pet Industry Trends to Watch in 2018 and Beyond. Retrieved from https://blog.marketresearch.com/4-pet-industry-trends-to-watch-in-2018-and-beyond

Smith, C. (2019). 250 Amazing Instagram Statistics. Retrieved from https://expandedramblings.com/index.php/important-instagram-stats/

Study: The most popular Instagram filters from around the world. (n.d.). Retrieved from https://www.canva.com/learn/popular-instagram-filters/

Taylor, C. (2012). Instagram Passes 50 Million Users, Adds 5 Million a Week. Retrieved from https://mashable.com/2012/04/30/instagram-50-million-users/

Top 10 Successful Hashtag Campaigns That Created an Impact. (2019). Retrieved from https://medium.com/@unboxsocial/top-10-successful-hashtag-campaigns-that-created-an-impact-3605f4d6e5fc

The Best Time to Post on Instagram By Day, Niche & More. (2019). Retrieved from https://www.sharethis.com/best-practices/2018/03/best-time-to-post-on-instagram/

US AD Spending. (2019). Retrieved from http://bluemoondigital.co/wp-content/uploads/2016/12/eMarketer_US_Ad_Spending-eMarketers_Updated_Estimates_and_Forecast_for_2015%E2%80%93_2020.pdf

Vrountas, T. (2018). Why Instagram Video Ads May Be a Good Fit for Your Brand. Retrieved from https://instapage.com/blog/instagram-video-ads

West, C. (2019). 17 Instagram stats marketers need to know for 2019. Retrieved from https://sproutsocial.com/insights/instagram-stats/